New+ GET UP TO SPEED

Situational

New Get Up to Speed + *Situational*
helps students learn how to speak like a native speaker by focusing on contemporary language usage in everyday situations supplemented with modern facts and cultural notions.

Key Features
- Warm Up Activity
- Useful Phrases
- Slang & Idioms
- Key Conversation
- Situational Collocations
- What Would You Do?
- Cultural Discussion Questions
- If You Ask Me

MP3

CARROT HOUSE

CARROT HOUSE

New Get Up To Speed+ 8 Situational
© Carrot House

All rights reserved. No part of this publication may be reproduced,
stores in a retrieval system, or transmitted in any form or by any means
without the prior permission in writing of Carrot House.

Printed : First published January 2019
Reprinted September 2019

Author : Carrot Language Lab

ISBN 978-89-6732-298-4

Printed and distributed in Korea
9F, 488, Gangnam St. Gangnam-gu, Seoul, 06120, South Korea

Curriculum Map

Course	Level 1	Level 2	Level 3	Level 4	Level 5	Level 6	Level 7	Text Book
General Conversation	Essential English : Begin Again							
	Pre Get Up to Speed 1~2							
		New Get Up to Speed+ 1~2						
			New Get Up to Speed+ 3~4					
				New Get Up to Speed+ 5~6				
					New Get Up to Speed+ 7~8			
	Daily Focused English 1							
		Daily Focused English 2						
Discussion			Active Discussion 1					
				Active Discussion 2				
					Dynamic Discussion			
			Chicken Soup Course					
				Dynamic Information & Digital Technology				
Business Conversation	Pre Business Basics 1							
		Pre Business Basics 2						
			Business Basics 1					
				Business Basics 2				
				Business Practice 1				
					Business Practice 2			
Global Biz Workshop				Effective Business Writing Skills (Workbook)				
				Effective Presentation Skills (Workbook)				
					Effective Negotiation Skills (Workbook)			
					Cross-Cultural Training 1~2 (Workbook)			
					Leadership Training Course (Workbook)			
Business Skills			Simple & Clear Technical Writing Skills					
				Effective Business Writing Skills				
				Effective Meeting Skills				
				Business Communication (Negotiation)				
				Effective Presentation Skills				
					Marketing 1			
						Marketing 2		
					Management			
On the Job English				Human Resources				
				Accounting and Finance				
				Marketing and Sales				
				Production Management				
				Automotive				
				Banking and Commerce				
				Medical and Medicine				
				Information Technology				
				Construction				
			Construction English in Use 1 ~ 4					
			Public Service English in Use					

※ This Curriculum Map illustrates the entire line-up of textbooks at CARROT HOUSE.

CARROT HOUSE_ 2019.01

Curriculum Map

New⁺ GET UP TO SPEED
Situational

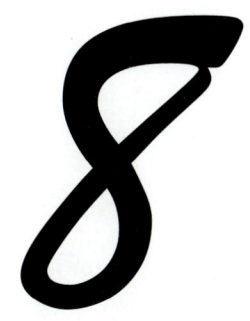

Introduction

Carrot House Methodology

Andragogical Approach & Productive English

The teaching of children (pedagogy) and adult learning (andragogy) are distinctively different. Pedagogy is akin to training and encourages convergent thinking and rote learning. It is compulsory, centered on the teacher and the imparting of information with minimal control by the learner. Andragogy, by contrast, is about education as freedom. It encourages divergent thinking and active learning. It is voluntary, learner oriented and opens up vistas for continual learning. Adults need to feel independent and in control of their learning. Therefore, Carrot House curriculum is based on andragogy and is designed to encourage learners' participation and engagement by providing more task-based activities and opportunities to frequently interact in the classroom. People want to achieve communicative competence when they learn other languages. English education in EFL environments has been rather focused on the receptive skills of English—listening and reading—which simply increases learners' knowledge about a language, not the competence of using it. If people are well equipped with productive skills—speaking and writing—they will be competent in English communication. This is why Carrot House curriculum is designed to enhance learners' productive skills throughout the course. This andragogical approach of the Carrot House Curriculum, which focuses on productive English, will enable learners to achieve communication skills necessary for global competence. Carrot House's teaching philosophy and curriculum combine to provide a "Language for Success" for all learners.

Communicative Language Learning (CLL)

This communicative interaction, the essential component of language acquisition, does not occur in a typical, non-meaningful, fun-oriented conversation with native speakers. It occurs in a negotiated interaction through which a well-trained teacher provides the comprehensible input that is appropriate to the learners. The learners, at the same time, actively utilize the opportunities given to them by the teachers. To this end, the Communicative Language Learning (CLL) method is employed in the field of Foreign Language Acquisition. The CLL method provides activities that are geared toward using language pragmatically, authentically and functionally with the intention of achieving meaningful purposes.

Course Overview

Features

Productive English
Learn to use practical and authentic expressions in various daily conversation, common collocations, written sentences, and activities.

Maximization of Schema
The use of visual texts, topic specific questions and useful expressions allow learners to find connections between the contents and their lives by maximizing their schema.

Interactive Activity
Activities, such as role-play, pair-work, group-work, and class-work, provide learners with the opportunity to constantly interact each other.

A Range of Everyday Topics
Through dealing with a range of daily situations in class, learners are equipped to tackle similar situations in reality.

Discussion
Learners can expand their ability to effectively express themselves in English through discussing a broad range of topics.

Slang / Idiom
Through learning topic-related slang and idioms, learners can improve their English language proficiency and use contemporary informal expressions to articulate their ideas.

Opinions on Topic-related Situations
Aims to enhance learner's abilities to speak logically. This task gives learners the chance to express their opinions on a given topic or from a choice of two situations.

Lesson Composition

Each New Get Up To Speed+ Situational book 5-8 is composed of 11 lessons.
Each lesson is composed of 8 main activities and 3 useful extra activities.

1. Warm Up Activity

To activate the students and their background knowledge, the lesson starts with discussing an image together with three situation-related-questions.

2. Useful Phrases

Students can improve and polish their English-language ability by practicing to integrate actively used phrases into their daily language.

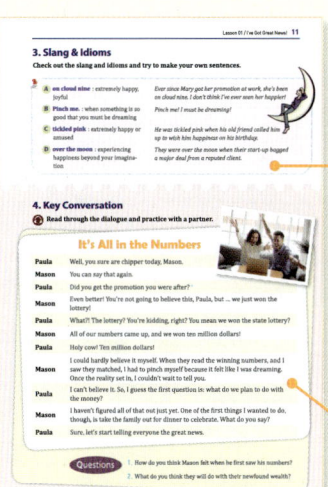

3. Slang & Idioms

Reinforce the learner's ability to speak English like a native through the use of situational contemporary slang & idioms.

4. Key Conversation

Students can read, listen, and repeat how native speakers communicate with others on a daily basis. The activity also includes questions to test comprehension skills.

5. Situational Collocations

Students can improve and polish their English-language ability by learning and practicing how native speakers commonly group everyday words.

Lesson Composition

Each New Get Up To Speed+ Situational book 5-8 is composed of 11 lessons.
Each lesson is composed of 8 main activities and 3 useful extra activities.

6. What Would You Do?

Students can improve their comprehension and English word analyzing and discussion skills through geared situations and questions. This helps students practice their language-use for a wide variety of situations.

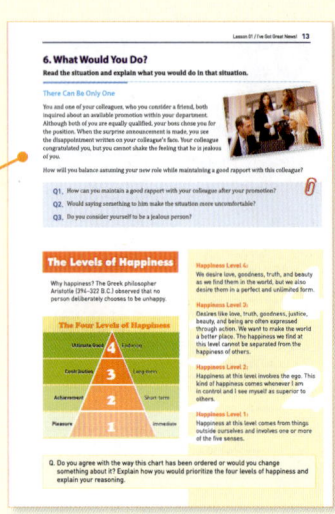

7. Cultural Discussion Questions

Gives the learners the opportunity to share, learn, and discuss global, cultural, and personal opinions and notions.

8. If You Ask Me

Gives the learners the opportunity to make a choice and share and defend their personal opinions of debatable issues.

Extra Activities

Each lesson includes three extra activities composed of engaging facts and figures. These activities provide students with both popular and intriguing global facts. These can also be used to help facilitate a more fun and enjoyable class.

Contents

Title	Learning Objective	Expression Check	
Lesson 1 I've Got Great News!	To express happiness regarding first time experiences.	- I can't believe this is really happening to someone like me. - Things like this just don't happen to me. - Things are finally starting to go my way for once.	10
Lesson 2 I Swear It's True	To discuss unrealistic events that really happened.	- Have you heard about this guy's near-death experience? - The odds were stacked against him, but he was a fighter. - It's hard to believe this child surived a plane crash.	16
Lesson 3 The Tabloids are Having a Field Day	To discuss celebrity news and other gossip.	- Did you hear the latest on…? - Do you think it's true that…? - Did you get a look at her outfit?	22
Lesson 4 A Bright Future	To discuss setbacks and future possibilities.	- Don't dwell on the past—the sky's the limit. - I'm up the creek without a paddle. - Don't look back. Onward and upward.	28
Lesson 5 Blowing Off Steam	To discuss methods for handling stress and anger.	- Maybe you should take a step back and remove yourself from the situation. - You have to stop letting things get to you like that. - Stop taking things so seriously.	34
Lesson 6 It Truly is a Small World	To discuss the positive and negative aspects of an increasingly globalized society.	- There's a real push these days for our country to be more globalized. - We're really part of one global village. - As the world becomes more globalized, foreign language skills are growing more important.	40
Lesson 7 The Dangers of Discrimination	To discuss various forms of discrimination that are present in modern society.	- It's obvious that there's a glass ceiling at this company. - People from that part of town are treated like second-class citizens. - That comment was borderline sexual harassment.	46
Lesson 8 Flattery Will Get You Nowhere	To offer and respond to flattery in personal and professional situations.	- I love that tie you're wearing. It really brings out your eyes. - You handled that like the true professional you are. - You do wonder for my ego.	52
Lesson 9 Dealing With Conflict	To discuss different methods for dealing with conflict.	- I tend to avoid conflict at all costs. - I prefer to take the bull by the horns. - Let's just agree to disagree.	58
Lesson 10 A Lost Passport	To cope with losing personal identification in a foreign country.	- I'm pretty sure I packed my passport, but I can't find it anywhere. - How am I supposed to drive when I misplaced my license? - Do you remember me putting my credit card back in my wallet?	64
Lesson 11 Job Satisfaction	To discuss the relationship between employers and their employees.	- Why do I have to wait around until the boss is ready to go home? - I've never understood why we have to do that. - My boss and I are finally seeing eye to eye on things.	70
Lesson 12 I'd Like to Report a Break-in	To discuss home invasions and how to prevent them.	- I think someone has just broken into my house. - They made off with everything. - The police have been dispatched to your location.	76

Slang & Idioms — 82

Answer Key — 84

01 I've Got Great News!

Learning Objective
Upon completion of this lesson you will be able to **express happiness regarding first time experiences.**

Expression Check
- ☑ I can't believe this is really happening to someone like me.
- ☑ Things like this just don't happen to me.
- ☑ Things are finally starting to go my way for once.

1. Warm Up Activity
Talk about the questions.

1. Describe a thrilling first-time experience that you have had.
2. Do the things that made you happy ten years ago still make you happy today?
3. Is there something that you have not done yet but really want to try?

2. Useful Phrases
Match the phrases (a-d) to the phrases (1-4) to form a complete sentence. The useful phrases are italicized.

A I was so happy,

B I can't believe things worked out so well!

C Things like that just don't happen to someone like me!

D *Things are finally starting to go my way.*

1 *I'm really counting my lucky stars.*

2 Everything in my life is just how I want it to be.

3 *I cried tears of joy.*

4 *It must be my lucky day!*

3. Slang & Idioms

Check out the slang and idioms and try to make your own sentences.

A	**on cloud nine** : extremely happy, joyful	*Ever since Mary got her promotion at work, she's been on cloud nine. I don't think I've ever seen her happier!*
B	**Pinch me.** : when something is so good that you must be dreaming	*Pinch me! I must be dreaming!*
C	**tickled pink** : extremely happy or amused	*He was tickled pink when his old friend called him up to wish him happiness on his birthday.*
D	**over the moon** : experiencing happiness beyond your imagination	*They were over the moon when their start-up bagged a major deal from a reputed client.*

4. Key Conversation

Read through the dialogue and practice with a partner.

It's All in the Numbers

Paula	Well, you sure are chipper today, Mason.
Mason	You can say that again.
Paula	Did you get the promotion you were after?
Mason	Even better! You're not going to believe this, Paula, but … we just won the lottery!
Paula	What?! The lottery? You're kidding, right? You mean we won the state lottery?
Mason	All of our numbers came up, and we won ten million dollars!
Paula	Holy cow! Ten million dollars!
Mason	I could hardly believe it myself. When they read the winning numbers, and I saw they matched, I had to pinch myself because it felt like I was dreaming. Once the reality set in, I couldn't wait to tell you.
Paula	I can't believe it. So, I guess the first question is: what do we plan to do with the money?
Mason	I haven't figured all of that out just yet. One of the first things I wanted to do, though, is take the family out for dinner to celebrate. What do you say?
Paula	Sure, let's start telling everyone the great news.

Questions

1. How do you think Mason felt when he first saw his numbers?
2. What do you think they will do with their newfound wealth?

I've Got Great News!

Tips on Finding Happiness

There are many different kinds of happiness. When you are feeling good, where do you think you fit in on this spectrum? This spectrum, which was written by a psychotherapist, supports people looking to live a happier, healthier, and more fulfilling life.

Q. Is the happiness you feel from interactions with your family different from the happiness you experience when you are with friends?

 **cheerful** — 56% of 30 to 45-year-olds say they are pretty happy

 **satisfied**

 gratified

 gleeful **peaceful** — 31% of 18 to 29-year-olds say they are very happy

 **overjoyed**

 playful — 29% of 46 to 64-year-olds say they are very happy

 **blissful** — 21% of 18 to 29 year-olds say helping others in need is one of the most important things in their lives

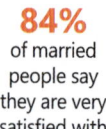 84% of married people say they are very satisfied with family life

 **jubilant**

 **excited** — 20% of people age 65 and up say they are 'not too happy'

 **comfortable** — 83% of Americans age 16 and up say they are very happy or pretty happy

 66% of single people say they are very satisfied with family life

 **proud**

5. Situational Collocations

Complete the sentences using the collocations from the word box.

Word Box

- happy dance
- purely by chance
- just what I needed
- extremely lucky
- significant breakthrough
- good fortune
- unexpected windfall
- financially free

1. With this new promotion, my family will finally be _____.
2. You bought me coffee? It's _____!
3. All it took was one _____ and his fortune was made.
4. This is _____, but I have an extra set that you can borrow.
5. Who do I thank for this _____?
6. The bonus I got last month was definitely an _____.
7. I did my _____ when I heard the good news.
8. The man was _____. All three people who came to his rescue were doctors.

6. What Would You Do?

Read the situation and explain what you would do in that situation.

There Can Be Only One

You and one of your colleagues, who you consider a friend, both inquired about an available promotion within your department. Although both of you are equally qualified, your boss chose you for the position. When the surprise announcement is made, you see the disappointment written on your colleague's face. Your colleague congratulated you, but you cannot shake the feeling that he is jealous of you.

How will you balance assuming your new role while maintaining a good rapport with this colleague?

Q1. How can you maintain a good rapport with your colleague after your promotion?

Q2. Would saying something to him make the situation more uncomfortable?

Q3. Do you consider yourself to be a jealous person?

The Levels of Happiness

Why happiness? The Greek philosopher Aristotle (394–322 B.C.) observed that no person deliberately chooses to be unhappy.

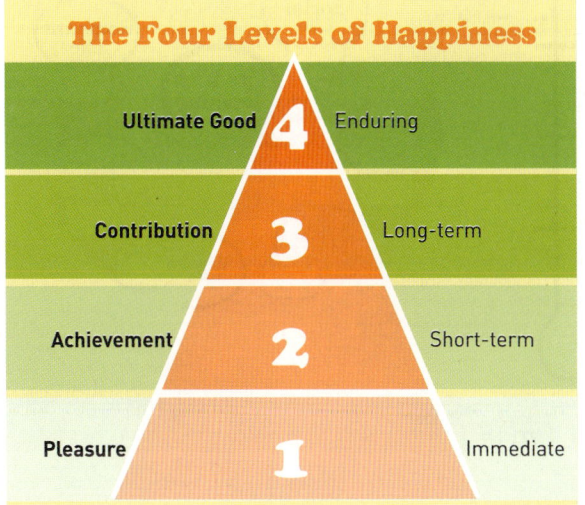

Happiness Level 4:
We desire love, goodness, truth, and beauty as we find them in the world, but we also desire them in a perfect and unlimited form.

Happiness Level 3:
Desires like love, truth, goodness, justice, beauty, and being are often expressed through action. We want to make the world a better place. The happiness we find at this level cannot be separated from the happiness of others.

Happiness Level 2:
Happiness at this level involves the ego. This kind of happiness comes whenever I am in control and I see myself as superior to others.

Happiness Level 1:
Happiness at this level comes from things outside ourselves and involves one or more of the five senses.

Q. Do you agree with the way this chart has been ordered or would you change something about it? Explain how you would prioritize the four levels of happiness and explain your reasoning.

I've Got Great News!

7. Cultural Discussion Questions

Read the passage and talk about the questions in as much detail as possible.

The Secret

Rhonda Byrnes's bestselling book, *The Secret*, appeals not only to self-help junkies but also to anyone who is seeking the key to a better life. In the book, she argues that in order to achieve our goals, we must visualize what we want and imagine it into being. This is called the law of attraction. The law states that like attracts like, and therefore, to obtain happiness, one must first adopt a happy disposition and think only happy thoughts. For instance, if you are desperate for a promotion at work, you must visualize yourself being promoted and assuming your new role. This idea directly contradicts the long-held physical law of magnetism, which states that opposites attract.

1. Which one of these conflicting laws takes precedence in your mind: the law of attraction or the physical law of magnetism? Why?
2. Are self-help books like *The Secret* popular in your country? Which have you read?

How Happy Are You?

Everyone talks about happiness, but nobody really knows how to measure it. Let's find out if your life has meaning.

Directions: Rate each of the seven statements on a scale of 1 to 10, with 1 being "terrible" and 10 being "wonderful." When you are finished, add up your scores and divide the total by 70 to get your final score. Compare your results to the thermometer to see how happy you are.

Happiness Zone-You are a very happy person! If you are interested in where you can improve, then take your lowest score and fine-tune it.

Content Zone-You are pretty content in your life overall. However, simply being content because others have far less success in life is not going to help you meet your happiness potential.

Distressed Zone-In this zone, there is a good chance you are having difficulty dealing with people. You probably find them frustrating. Your expectations of life are not lining up to what you hoped for. Your first step should be to focus and try to improve.

Frustrated Zone-People in this zone attract other people that increase their frustration and worry. You are overwhelmed and weighed down with worry and anxiety.

Desperate Zone-This is the most dangerous zone. People in this zone have lost their peace of mind. Crying yourself to sleep at night is common. Chances are that you are in trouble financially and have health problems.

Q. How can you motivate yourself to be happier?

ALL YOU EVER REALLY WANTED

- **School Life**: To gain knowledge and skills in order to earn more and live a better life
- **Social Life**: To feel accepted with people of likeminded interests and values
- **Romantic Life**: To feel intimacy, importance and acceptance
- **Financial Life**: To be free from worries with a secure future and nicer things in life now
- **Married Life**: To maintain a daily normal life and be happy with a good relationship
- **Kids Life**: To help them grow up and be happy productive citizens
- **Work Life**: To be good at something that others will gladly pay for so you can live in the way you are accustomed

Life With Meaning — Peace Of Mind — All your experiences have value to others and you leave behind what really matters.

Thermometer zones:
- Happiness Zone (100°–80°)
- Content Zone (80°–60°)
- Distressed Zone (60°–50°)
- Frustrated Zone (50°–30°)
- Desperate Zone (20°–10°)

Your Score ☐ / Top Score (70) = Final Score ☐

8. If You Ask Me

Read the discussion topic and select the statement that you believe in the most. Then role-play the scenario.

Fate, Luck, or Opportunity?

On Maslow's Hierarchy of Needs, the idea of total happiness is called being self-actualized – an idea that a person has achieved complete fulfillment in every aspect of his/her life. In other doctrines, this idea is known as nirvana, euphoria, or Zen. All of these ideas share the common thread that ultimate happiness requires work. But it was the Roman philosopher Seneca who said, *"Luck is what happens when preparation meets opportunity."* Therefore, what role do you believe opportunity or fate plays in the pursuit of happiness?

Topic Question

Do you think happiness takes work (supportive), or is it a simple matter of fate (non-supportive)?

Supportive Opinion

VS

Non-Supportive Opinion

Role-play

Act out the role-play using the slang and idioms and useful expressions.

Situation
You and your friend are reflecting on your 20s. During this decade, both of you underwent many changes as you adjusted from student life to professional life. Your friend asks you how your life has changed since the day you turned 20. Discuss all the exciting things that you did in your 20s and beyond.

Role A
- Tell your friend about some of the things that you did since turning 20.
- Explain how you have changed as a person.

Role B
- Talk about how your life changed in your 20s.
- Describe how you feel about that time in your life.

Wrapping Up! Tell four things that you learned from this lesson and review.

1.　　　　　　2.　　　　　　3.　　　　　　4.

02 I Swear It's True

Learning Objective
Upon completion of this lesson you will be able to **discuss unrealistic events that really happened.**

Expression Check
- ☑ Have you heard about this guy's near-death experience?
- ☑ The odds were stacked against him, but he was a fighter.
- ☑ It's hard to believe this child survived a plane crash.

1. Warm Up Activity
Talk about the questions.

1. Has anything ever happened to you that you could not explain?
2. Do you believe that there is more to life than just our physical bodies?
3. Do you know anyone who has miraculously healed from a disease?

2. Useful Phrases
Match the phrases (a-d) to the phrases (1-4) to form a complete sentence. The useful phrases are italicized.

A. *Have you heard about*

B. *The odds were stacked against him,*

C. *It's hard to believe*

D. *I wouldn't believe it either,*

1. had I not seen it with my own eyes.
2. but *he was a fighter*.
3. this child survived a plane crash.
4. this guy's near-death experience?

Lesson 02 / I Swear It's True 17

3. Slang & Idioms
Check out the slang and idioms and try to make your own sentences.

A	**one in a million** : a chance that is extremely unlikely	We will know more in a month but so far, the scientists are guessing the odds at one in a million.
B	**near-death experience** : an experience described by some people who have been close to death	For some people, a near-death experience prompts a serious rethink.
C	**work miracles** : achieve extraordinary results, especially in trying to improve a situation	A balanced diet together with a gentle exercise regime can work miracles.
D	**not a chance** : not possible	Me lend you money? Not a chance!

4. Key Conversation

 Read through the dialogue and practice with a partner.

The Odds, One in a Million

Nelson	How's he doing, Doctor Gladstone?
Doctor	Well, to be completely honest, it's hard to believe he's still alive. From the reports I received about the accident, he's lucky to have survived.
Nelson	But is he going to be all right?
Doctor	Well, we're not in the clear yet. The odds are still stacked against him, and there might be some permanent damage if he does make it, but we'll do everything we can.
Nelson	So, what I hear you saying is you might not be able to save my son?
Doctor	Well, I'm no miracle worker, Mr. Nelson, but if I know your son, he's a fighter. I bet he'll pull through, even if the odds are one in a million.
Nelson	Thanks, Doc. It means a lot to hear you say that. Well, I guess it can't be helped. All we can do now is wait, right?
Doctor	Exactly. And pray for his recovery.
Nelson	Pray? I never knew you were so religious, Doctor.
Doctor	I wouldn't believe in it either, had I not seen it work with my own eyes. Besides, it couldn't hurt to try, right?

Questions
1. How would you evaluate the boy's condition based on what you learned from the dialogue?
2. Do you think the Nelsons will follow the doctor's advice about praying for their son?

I Swear It's True

Absurd Movie Scenes That Actually Happened

We sometimes watch movies because we want to see things that could never happen in real life – but the fact is that some of those moments actually did happen.

Absurd Scene #1 Mission: Impossible – Rappelling from the Ceiling

The Absurd Scene : The Reality :

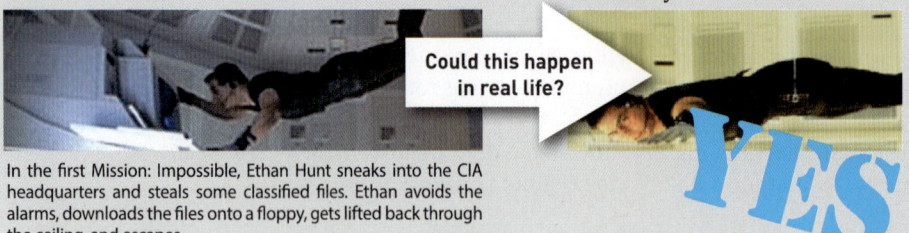

In the first Mission: Impossible, Ethan Hunt sneaks into the CIA headquarters and steals some classified files. Ethan avoids the alarms, downloads the files onto a floppy, gets lifted back through the ceiling, and escapes.

A few years ago, a group of highly organized professional thieves used the exact same method as Ethan Hunt to rob a Best Buy in New Jersey. According to police, they climbed an exterior pipe and removed a piece of the roof using a suction device. At that point, they rappelled into the store, staying 10 feet off the ground at all times -- any lower would have triggered the store's alarm.

Absurd Scene #2 Goldfinger – James Bond Has a Tuxedo Under His Wetsuit

The Absurd Scene :

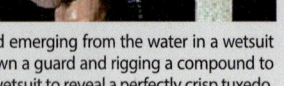

Goldfinger begins with Bond emerging from the water in a wetsuit and then, after knocking down a guard and rigging a compound to explode, Bond removes his wetsuit to reveal a perfectly crisp tuxedo.

It's impossible!

Q1 What other absurd scenes do you remember from movies? Do you think they could actually happen in real life?

Q2 What are the most absurd things that have happened in your life?

5. Situational Collocations

Complete the sentences using the collocations from the word box.

Word Box

- mind-blowing ending
- beyond reason
- implausible story
- unthinkable coincidence
- bewildering explanation
- no small feat
- unlikely chain of events
- statistically improbable

1. The accident set off an _____ that scientists still struggle to explain to this day.
2. After listening to his _____, the police decided to investigate.
3. Although it seems _____, all passengers survived the crash.
4. It's an _____ that he showed up at exactly the right moment.
5. Angered _____, I ran into the bedroom and packed a bag to leave.
6. Getting them to agree to the terms of the contract was a _____.
7. She initially tried to defend her controversial stance with a _____ on Twitter.
8. Just listen and wait, because this story has a _____.

6. What Would You Do?

Read the situation and explain what you would do in that situation.

A Terrible Accident

You planned to meet a friend at a café for lunch, but your friend did not show up on time. You are annoyed and call your friend twice and finally eat on your own and leave. Later in the day, you hear some of your peers discussing a terrible accident that happened during the lunch break near your office, and your friend's name is mentioned as one of the people hurt in the accident. You hurt to the hospital to check on your friend and learn from the doctor that he/she is lucky to be alive.

Q1. Thirty minutes pass and your friend still hasn't shown up yet, what would you do?

Q2. After waiting at the hospital, you can finally get to see your friend. What would you say to him/her?

Q3. Have you ever experienced a shocking incident like this? What did you do?

Unbelievable Things that **Happen Every 60** Seconds on the Internet

A lot can happen in a minute! Amazing things happen instantly on the internet. Until recently, no one could ever imagine so many things could happen so quickly! Every 60 seconds, there are over 695,000 Facebook status updates – imagine how many there are by the end of the day. Apart from that 4,000 USB devices are sold, 12 websites are hacked, 232 computers are infected with malware, and over 950 sales close on eBay. Can you think of any other amazing things that happen in just 60 seconds?

Q1. What did you do in the last minute/hour/day of your life?

Q2. Tell about something exciting that you have learned recently.

I Swear It's True

7. Cultural Discussion Questions

Read the passage and talk about the questions in as much detail as possible.

Life after Death

Throughout the history of human civilization, people have long been fascinated by theories about what happens after death. In the Eastern religions of Hinduism and Buddhism, people believe that the soul is immortal and that we all will be reborn again into a new body after death. In the Western religions of Judaism, Christianity, and Islam, it is believed each person has only one life to live and based on our actions in life, the person's spirit will either live on eternally in paradise or suffer in hell. Some newer religions blend these two ideas into a mixture of reincarnated bliss, while some atheists choose to believe that death is simply the end. Occasionally, people who have suffered near-death experiences claim that they have seen paradise, but no one knows for sure what lies ahead once our spirits pass on.

1. What do you believe happens after death?
2. Do you think people who claim to have seen the afterlife during near-death experiences are telling the truth? Why or why not?

Making the Impossible Possible

The images below illustrate that even a possible project can become impossible if those involved fail to plan and adequately communicate their goals to others involved.

So, what can we do to make sure projects stay on track?

#1. Ensure a qualified, capable, and committed project team is in place, with clearly defined roles, responsibilities, ownership, and accountability.

#2. Set realistic business objectives and continuously manage stakeholders' expectations.

#3. Understand project requirements and specifications.

#4. Communicate, communicate, communicate.

#5. Add enough contingency to your work timescale.

How the customer explained it

How the project leader understood it

How the engineer designed it

How the programmer wrote it

How the sales executive described it

How the project was documented

What operations installed

How the customer was billed

How the helpdesk supported it

What the customer really needed

Q1 Have you ever done something that you originally thought to be impossible? What was it? How did you accomplish your goal?

Q2 Some people argue that nothing is truly impossible if you put your mind to it. Do you agree or disagree? What are some truly impossible things that you have encountered in your life?

8. If You Ask Me

Read the discussion topic and select the statement that you believe in the most. Then role-play the scenario.

Healed by Faith

Many ancient cultures believed in the practice of faith healing. Even in the modern day, major religions also share the view that fatal diseases can be healed by prayer or by demonstrating good actions. Sometimes, individuals claiming to have a special healing "gift" are able to gain a following and profit from the desperation of those seeking a cure. Although faith healing sometimes appears to be effective in some cases, often no matter how much a person prays for relief from their illness, their health continues to deteriorate. Although some research has demonstrated a link between mental, physical, and spiritual health, false healers and disappointing experiences have cast a shadow of doubt over whether faith healing should be viewed as a valid cure.

Topic Question

Do you believe that faith healing is possible, or is it just a superstition left over from a more primitive time?

Supportive Opinion VS **Non-Supportive Opinion**

Role-play

Act out the role-play using the slang and idioms and useful expressions.

Situation

You just watched a television special about a boy who was declared dead for almost an hour following a car accident. After miraculously coming back to life, he claimed that he had visited Heaven during the time he was assumed to be dead. He provided many specific details and you feel that his account was very reliable. You are very excited to hear this proof that there is a life after death. Call your best friend and share with him or her what you have learned.

Role A
- Tell your friend you have exciting news.
- Explain what you saw on TV.

Role B
- Tell your friend that you are skeptical.
- Say that you have heard stories like that are a result of oxygen deprivation to the brain.

Wrapping Up!

Tell four things that you learned from this lesson and review.

1.
2.
3.
4.

03 The Tabloids Are **Having a Field Day**

Learning Objective
Upon completion of this lesson, you will be able to **discuss celebrity news and other gossip.**

Expression Check
- ☑ Did you hear the latest on…?
- ☑ Do you think it's true that…?
- ☑ Did you get a look at her outfit?

1. Warm Up Activity
Talk about the questions.

1. Who is your favorite celebrity or famous person, and why?
2. Are you interested in the lives of the rich and famous? Why or why not?
3. What do you think are the advantages and disadvantages of being a celebrity?

2. Useful Phrases
Match the phrases (a-d) to the phrases (1-4) to form a complete sentence. The useful phrases are italicized.

A. *Did you hear the latest on*

B. *Do you think it's true that*

C. *Did you get a look at*

D. The paparazzi *just don't care at all about*

1. he embezzled all that money?
2. her outfit? Ridiculous, right?
3. the harassment scandal?
4. personal privacy.

3. Slang & Idioms

Check out the slang and idioms and try to make your own sentences.

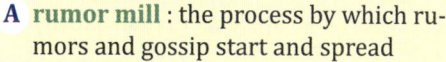

A **rumor mill** : the process by which rumors and gossip start and spread	*During times of uncertainty, the rumor mill turns faster than ever.*
B **star-studded** : including many famous people	*But overall, the event was a star-studded night with Hollywood and Washington's elite.*
C **having a field day** : busy doing something that they enjoy	*Journalists are having a field day with the current political scandal.*
D **15 minutes of fame** : a short lived media publicity or celebrity	*Aspiring social celebrities are constantly looking for their 15 minutes of fame.*

4. Key Conversation

Read through the dialogue and practice with a partner.

A Star-Studded Evening

Clarissa Hey, did you catch the Oscars last night? It sure was a star-studded evening.

Layla Of course! Did you happen to see Rebecca Law's outfit? I really wonder what she was wearing—wish I could pull that off.

Clarissa Do you think it's true that she's married to Timothy Penn now? I mean, the rumor mill has been churning, and they're all over the glossies this month.

Layla The press sure is having a field day with them. The paparazzi just don't care at all about a person's privacy. I saw a nasty picture of her getting on a bus without a lick of makeup and speculation about a baby bump.

Clarissa At any rate, I sure don't envy them. I bet they're always fighting off the fans everywhere they go. Have you seen her new line of clothing up at the mall? All the proceeds are going to feed the hungry in Africa.

Layla Figures she'd be doing something great to boost her image. I do like her style, though.

Questions
1. Are you interested in celebrity fashion like Layla?
2. Do you think Law and Penn have an easy life?

The Tabloids are Having a Field Day

Do Women Really Gossip More than Men?

It was reported by the Social Issues Research Center that gossip accounts for 55% of men's conversation time and 67% of women's, a much smaller gap between the two genders than usually thought.

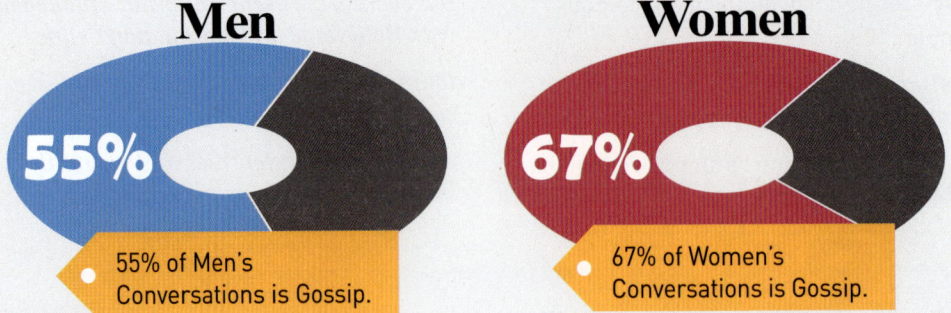

- 55% of Men's Conversations is Gossip.
- 67% of Women's Conversations is Gossip.

So why do so many people assume that women gossip more than men? Is it because women are not as discreet about it? Or is it that they have a wider range of tone inflection so it is more obvious? Some would argue that men discuss subjects considered more important, including politics. As one psychologist wrote, *"It is said that women gossip more than men do. Perhaps they only do it better. Men just call it 'networking.' Men are much more interested in who is up and who is down. Women tend to gossip more about who's in and who has merit."*

Q1 Why do you think people love to gossip about others?

Q2 When was the last time you gossiped? Who did you gossip with?

5. Situational Collocations

Complete the sentences using the collocations from the word box.

Word Box

- story going around
- rumor has it
- vicious rumor
- unfounded suspicion
- unsubstantiated allegations
- malicious gossip
- keep this to yourself
- acting scandalously

1. There's a _____ that he was fired from the hit drama.
2. _____, but I hear that's not his real hair.
3. I can't believe the magazine published such a _____.
4. Once I got home from work, I quickly discovered that it was an _____.
5. During a press conference, the singer quickly dismissed the stories as _____.
6. _____ the pair eloped over the weekend.
7. The Oscar winner was reportedly _____ at the event.
8. I wouldn't put it past him to spread _____ about you.

6. What Would You Do?

Read the situation and explain what you would do in that situation.

Celebrity Spotting

You and your sister are having dinner at a local restaurant. You notice someone who looks familiar. You realize the man is a famous actor from a new TV show that you just started watching. He is by himself, so you wonder if it would be appropriate for you to go over, introduce yourself, and ask for an autograph. You mention this idea to your sibling and she says that she thinks it would be a violation of his personal privacy to do so.

- Q1. Would you disregard your sibling's advice and ask anyway?
- Q2. What would you say if you approached the actor?
- Q3. Have you ever seen a celebrity in person? Who was it? What did you do?

How Different Blood Types Gossip

Type A points out others' weaknesses intelligently.

Type A speaks negatively of others behind their backs, even though he does not look like he would gossip.

Type A is afraid that others will find out that he spoke badly about them.

Type B does not really know much about many things.

Type O uses explosive language.

Type AB is not easily influenced and stays cool.

- Q1. What blood type are you? Do you feel like this analysis is accurate?
- Q2. If someone found out that you spoke negatively about them, how would you react?

The Tabloids are Having a Field Day

7. Cultural Discussion Questions

Read the passage and talk about the questions in as much detail as possible.

Tabloid Magazines

In the US, grocery check-out lines are framed by rows of impulse-buy items, often including tabloid magazines or weekly papers. Covers are always eye-catching, and they feature stories that are sensational, shocking, and speculative. Our eyes are often attracted to these glossies even though many people think they are garbage. Things such as pregnancies, weddings, drug and alcohol problems, weight gain, and scandals are often exploited by these publications for a quick profit.

1. Do you have tabloids in your country? What do you think of them?
2. Are celebrities in your country good role models for the younger generation?

How Accurate Are Tabloids?

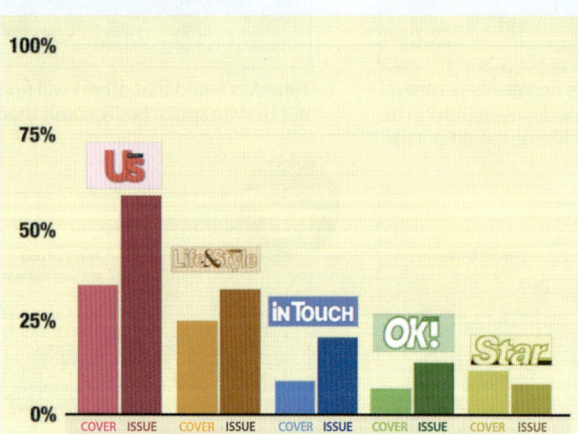

Now the results are in...

- **US Weekly** – **35%** cover story accuracy, **59%** overall accuracy.
- **Style** – **25%** cover story accuracy, **34%** overall accuracy.
- **In Touch** – **9%** cover story accuracy, **21%** overall accuracy.
- **OK!** – **7%** cover story accuracy, **14%** overall accuracy.
- **Star** – **9%** cover story accuracy, **12%** overall accuracy.

A recent survey took 20 months' worth of what are known as **"falsifiable rumors"** – break-ups, marriages, pregnancies, engagements, adoptions, and reconciliations – in five major celebrity-driven magazines to find out which was the most accurate.

Q. Do you believe most of what you read in the tabloids? Why or why not?

8. If You Ask Me

Read the discussion topic and select the statement that you believe in the most. Then role-play the scenario.

Paparazzi Rights

With the tragic death of Princess Diana, the spotlight was shone brightly on the paparazzi and their tactics of capturing the stars' lives. Some strongly support the right of the paparazzi to work freely on public property and even believe they should be able to use aggressive tactics to get a good shot. Others believe that there should be stricter laws regulating the activities of opportunist photographers in order to protect their subjects.

Topic Question

Do you think the paparazzi's rights should outshine those of the rich and famous?

Supportive Opinion

VS

Non-Supportive Opinion

Role-play

Act out the role-play using the slang and idioms and useful expressions.

Situation
During your lunch break, you check out your favorite entertainment news site and you stumble across some interesting gossip. Tell your co-worker about the rumor (marriage, baby, addition, etc.) that you just learned about and ask his or her opinion about the situation.

Role A
- Tell about an interesting thing that you have found out recently about a celebrity.
- Ask your co-worker what he or she thinks.

Role B
- Explain how you feel about the topic.
- Share some other entertainment gossip you've heard with your co-worker.

Wrapping Up! Tell four things that you learned from this lesson and review.

| 1 | 2 | 3 | 4 |

04 A Bright Future

Learning Objective
Upon completion of this lesson you will be able to **discuss setbacks and future possibilities.**

Expression Check
☑ Don't dwell on the past—the sky's the limit.
☑ I'm up the creek without a paddle.
☑ Don't look back. Onward and upward.

1. Warm Up Activity
Talk about the questions.

1. What would you do if you lost your job today?
2. What advice would you give a friend who is going through hard times?
3. If you got word that your spouse was transferred to another city, what adjustments would you need to make?

2. Useful Phrases
Match the phrases (a-d) to the phrases (1-4) to form a complete sentence. The useful phrases are italicized.

A Don't *dwell on the past*-

B I'm *up the creek*

C *Don't look back.*

D Just *view this as an opportunity*

1 to *reevaluate your priorities* in life.

2 the sky's the limit.

3 Onward and upward!

4 without a paddle.

3. Slang & Idioms

Check out the slang and idioms and try to make your own sentences.

A	**be laid off** : losing one's job because a company lacks work or funds to pay your salary	*He was laid off last year when his company merged with another.*
B	**Things are falling into place.** : used when things are happening in a satisfactory way, without problems	*It's been a hard year, but finally, things are falling into place for me.*
C	**temporary setback** : a defeat or reverse of progress	*Don't worry about it so much. It's just a temporary setback.*
D	**down in the dumps** : in a gloomy or depressed mood	*Nina seems to be down in the dumps because she broke up with her boyfriend recently.*

4. Key Conversation

Read through the dialogue and practice with a partner.

It's Just a Temporary Setback

Tabitha Marcus, hey, I'm so sorry to hear—I had no idea Robertson was so heartless—and right before the holidays, too!

Marcus I guess I kind of saw it coming. What am I going to do, Tabitha? I've got a wife and three kids, and we've already run right through our savings just trying to make ends meet. I know it's cliché, but I feel like I'm up the creek without a paddle.

Tabitha Hey, don't look back. Onward and upward, right? Don't dwell on the past. It's just a temporary setback. The sky's the limit for a young talent like you. Someone will hire you before you know it.

Marcus I guess I should just view this as an opportunity to reevaluate my priorities in life. Maybe I'm not doing what I'm supposed to be doing, you know?

Tabitha Yeah, these are tough times. Try to stay optimistic, be flexible, and keep your eyes open. I've got a friend who might know of a few position openings.

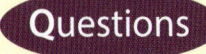

Questions

1. What happened to Marcus, and what do you think he should do today when he leaves the office?

2. How do you think Marcus is feeling now?

A Bright Future

5 Ways to Deal with Setbacks

$$\frac{\text{UPSET}}{\text{SETBACK}} = \text{STEP-UP}$$

KNOW THE	DIFFERENCE
SET BACK	FAILURE
YOU SLIPPED UP SCREWED UP LOST FOCUS CAVED GAVE IN GOT BUSY OR DISTRACTED YOURSELF	YOU DECIDED YOUR HEALTH WAS NOT WORTH THE EFFORT

Setbacks are an important part of life. They are a part of trying anything new, a part of our growth as human beings, and a part of the human condition. If any skill is worth learning, it is how to learn from a setback.

Setbacks Are Not Failures
The difference between a setback and a failure is just a matter of perspective. When describing something as a setback, we put ourselves in a position to start again.

Embrace the Setbacks
Imagine if you could live without a single setback. What would that be like? The reality is that you would have never tried anything new.

Budget for Setbacks
Especially if you are starting on a completely new project, you should expect setbacks.

Keep Your Goals in Mind
Another way to budget for setbacks is to budget the time and energy you spend recovering from them. Learning from our mistakes is important.

Learning from Setbacks
Scheduling time to deal with setbacks and not dwelling on them when working on other projects will help you to complete your daily goals and also give your setbacks the time and energy required to deal with them.

Follow the Curve
Setbacks are directly proportional to the learning curve of doing new activities.

Q1 What were the most important lessons you have learned from your setbacks?

Q2 What opportunities were there after your setbacks?

5. Situational Collocations

Complete the sentences using the collocations from the word box.

Word Box

- gave me insight
- fall into depression
- put on a brave face
- process this information
- a range of emotions
- coping strategy
- bury your feelings
- grieve the loss

1. After a large disappointment, many people _____.
2. He _____ and confronted his boss.
3. It's important that you move on and don't _____.
4. Avoidance is a common _____ people use when faced with difficult problems.
5. I think I need more time to _____.
6. Try to _____ and move on.
7. Mark felt _____ following his divorce.
8. Losing my job _____ into what I really wanted to do with my life.

6. What Would You Do?

Read the situation and explain what you would do in that situation.

An Opportunity Abroad

Your spouse has been offered a new position at a branch office located in the US, but he/she has not accepted it yet and wants your opinion. He/she seems skeptical about making such a move, but you want to point out how it could positively impact your future and that of your children.

Q1. What might some benefits of moving abroad be?

Q2. What could you say to your spouse to convince him or her that this will be a positive change?

Q3. If you had the chance to relocate to another country, would you take it? Why?

What might some benefits of moving abroad be?

The Opportunity of Your Life

You have an opportunity right now, on this very day, that you will never have again.

The moments that make up this day are moments you can use to solve problems, to develop more effective ways of doing things, and to create value. The moments that make up this day are moments you could be using right now to move your life forward.

Look around you. See and appreciate what a magnificent world you live in and what a tremendous opportunity you have to make a difference.

The opportunity of your life is here.

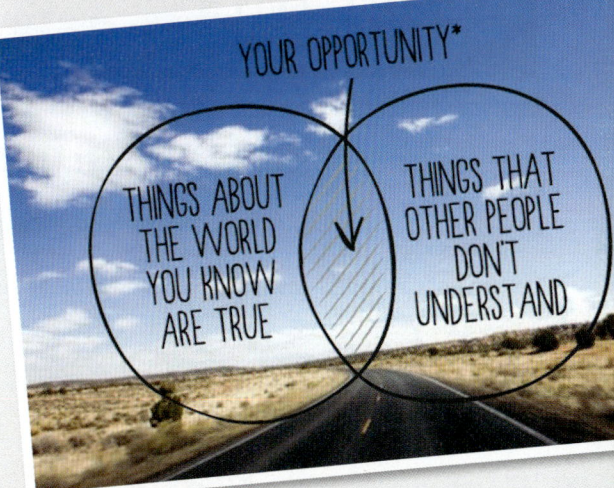

Q1 What does the word "opportunity" mean to you? Explain.

Q2 What do you consider when deciding whether to seize an opportunity?

A Bright Future

7. Cultural Discussion Questions

Read the passage and talk about the questions in as much detail as possible.

A Brighter Future

In the US, there has been a surge in the enrollment of older adults in post-secondary educational programs. Some adults go back to school in order to prepare for a career change. Others are looking for a way to stay competitive and boost their credentials. Education is viewed as a lifelong endeavor and a means to dramatically increase one's future opportunities.

1. How do people view mid-life career changes in your culture?
2. In your opinion, do the potential benefits of returning to school outweigh the costs in your country? Explain.

Setbacks as a Secret Weapon

Earning Power
Comparing Visionaries to Non-Visionaries

Super achievers have a goal, a vision of what they want to achieve and a role model of the person they want to be.

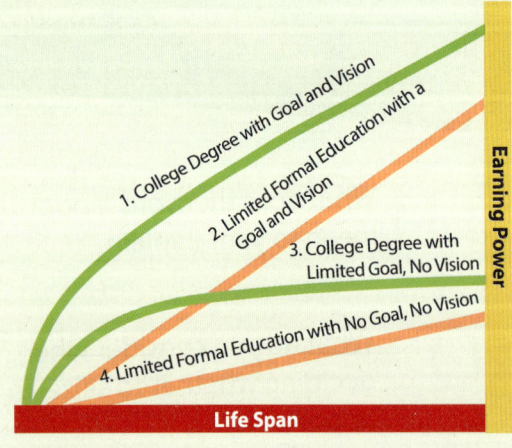

1. College Degree with Goal and Vision
2. Limited Formal Education with a Goal and Vision
3. College Degree with Limited Goal, No Vision
4. Limited Formal Education with No Goal, No Vision

Earning Power / Life Span

Q1. Where do you see yourself on the scale? Why?

Q2. Do you agree about the importance of having goals and a vision of what you want to achieve?

Lesson 4 / A Bright Future   33

8. If You Ask Me

Read the discussion topic and select the statement that you believe in the most. Then role-play the scenario.

A Risky Venture

In your city, more and more people are choosing to open small businesses as a means to a better future. There are a lot of rapidly developing neighborhoods where businesses are popping up and people are able to quickly turn a profit. However, success is far from guaranteed. Some areas eventually turn into virtual ghost towns full of empty storefronts and "for rent" signs. Going into business for yourself may seem like a viable option, but there are risks involved as well.

Topic Question

Taking into consideration the current economic and social climate of your city, would you consider going into business for yourself?

Supportive Opinion

VS

Non-Supportive Opinion

Role-play

Act out the role-play using the slang and idioms and useful expressions.

Situation
Your co-worker is looking a little down in the dumps today. You ask what is wrong and find out that he or she has once again been passed over for a promotion. This time it went to someone much younger and as a result, his or her future at the company feels hopeless. Offer some advice and encouragement about how your co-worker can gain the skills necessary to advance his or her career.

Role A
- Console him/her about the setback.
- Suggest taking classes to gain more skills to improve his or her chances at a promotion.

Role B
- Tell about your situation.
- Thank your co-worker for his or her help.

Wrapping Up!

Tell four things that you learned from this lesson and review.

1.   2.   3.   4.

05 Blowing Off Steam

Learning Objective
Upon completion of this lesson you will be able to **discuss methods for handling stress and anger.**

Expression Check
- ☑ Maybe you should take a step back and remove yourself from the situation.
- ☑ You have to stop letting things get to you like that.
- ☑ Stop taking things so seriously.

1. Warm Up Activity
Talk about the questions.

1. Do you think that stress can ever have a positive effect? Why or why not?
2. How does stress usually affect you?
3. What are some things you do to relieve stress?

2. Useful Phrases
Match the phrases (a-d) to the phrases (1-4) to form a complete sentence. The useful phrases are italicized.

A Maybe you *should take a step back*

B You have to

C *Forget about it.* You need to

D I can't commit to that now.

1 stop letting things get to you like that.

2 I've *got too much on my plate* as it is.

3 stop taking things so seriously.

4 and *remove yourself from the situation.*

Lesson 05 / Blowing Off Steam

3. Slang & Idioms

Check out the slang and idioms and try to make your own sentences.

A	**let off steam** : get rid of pent-up energy or strong emotion	I really need to take some time to relax and let off some steam.
B	**stressed out** : tired and irritable because of too much work or pressure	With the quarterly sales report due, the whole team's been stressed out this week.
C	**at one's wits' end** : at the limits of one's emotional or mental limitations	The family has been at their wits' end trying to ensure somebody answers for this.
D	**between a rock and a hard place** : in a situation where one is faced with two equally difficult alternatives	As an investor, you are between a rock and a hard place if your company faces bankruptcy.

4. Key Conversation

Read through the dialogue and practice with a partner.

Take a Chill Pill

Chantel Seriously, can you believe that guy?

Jackson Who are you talking about?

Chantel Jacob. I mean, he knows that we're overworked right now as it is, what with Christmas coming and all. I'm already at my wits' end trying to figure out the ads for the new line-up, and now he pulls this on us?

Jackson What did he do this time?

Chantel He went and booked a whole week off for himself during our busiest season. That means more work for the rest of us. I can't handle any more of his junk. I've got a lot on my plate as it is.

Jackson OK, Chantel. Take a chill pill, all right? You have to stop letting things like that get to you so much. You know he's been under a lot of pressure, too, right?

Chantel Oh, so now you're taking his side?

Jackson No. I just think he's smart for taking a step back and removing himself from the situation. Maybe we should follow his example, you know? It might help clear our heads.

Questions

1. Do you think Chantel is justified in being angry about Jacob's behavior?
2. Do you think Jackson's advice is wise, given their situation?

Blowing Off Steam

5. Situational Collocations

Complete the sentences using the collocations from the word box.

Word Box

- undue stress
- enough hours in the day
- common theme
- relinquish control
- make time for
- identify the source
- pare down
- debilitating anxiety

1. You need to _____ relaxation in your busy schedule.
2. I'm making a conscious effort to _____ my responsibilities in the office.
3. There aren't _____ to deal with this problem.
4. I noticed that she really struggles with _____ of the small details.
5. I have dark circles and wrinkles from at least four years of _____.
6. A _____ in my life is the pursuit of fast success.
7. You must first _____ of your stress.
8. She had to take some time off work to deal with her _____.

Manage Your Anger Addiction

Dealing with anger is especially difficult when outbursts of rage happen again and again. These patterns are hard to stop, and the results can be devastating to all those involved. The diagram below illustrates the endlessly repeating cycle of anger addiction.

The Cycle of Anger Addiction

- Things just do not feel right. You are not getting what you want.
- You have done everything you can, and it is not any better.
- Your frustration and pain are building up inside, but you are not talking about it.
- You are getting madder and madder inside, and it just gets stronger.
- You are feeling stressed and irritated, and your fuse is getting shorter.
- You feel a little relief after you blow up, like a pressure has lifted.
- The ones you hurt are probably the people you love. You promised you would not do it again.
- You feel bad for hurting and scaring them, but you may not be good at apologizing. Even if you apologize, it does not seem to help. They do not believe you.
- You probably think you were right or somehow justified with your anger.
- Ultimately, you are not feeling any better than before. You are still not getting what you need.
- The anger might even be worse. You had your blowup, so you feel some relief from the built-up pressure inside.

Q1. Tell about the last time that you felt uneasy about something. How did you respond to the problem?

Q2. How do you usually manage your stress when confronted with difficult situations? Explain.

6. What Would You Do?

Read the situation and explain what you would do in that situation.

Between a Rock and a Hard Place

It's the busiest time of the year for your company. You have several deadlines coming up and your office is full of activity. There is a lot of pressure from the CEO to perform well. As a result, there has been a lot of staff turnover lately, with HR cracking down on people who can't perform well under pressure. Suddenly, your supervisor tells you that he will be going on vacation for two weeks starting tomorrow. He has reassigned all of his work to you. It is fine for him to do so because his position at the company is secure, but you have no idea how you will be able to cope with all the extra work. You feel resentful that he is able to take a break during such a busy time.

Q1. How would you respond to the situation?
Q2. What could you do to relieve stress?
Q3. Who would you go to for advice in this situation?

The Dangers of Stress

Not all stress is bad. Good stress can motivate workers to stretch themselves and meet a new challenge. However, stress is still a major issue for many employees.

Main Causes of Stress

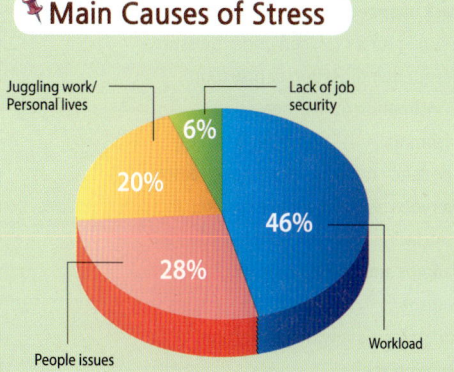

- Juggling work/Personal lives — 20%
- Lack of job security — 6%
- Workload — 46%
- People issues — 28%

Stress Takes a Toll

51% — 51% of employees say they have high levels of stress, with extreme fatigue/feeling out of control.

50% — 50% of employees miss one to two days of work per year due to stress.

46% — 46% of employees surveyed say they come to work one to four days a year when they are too stressed to be effective.

How Employees Deal with Stress

57% — 57% of Generation Y employees take unplanned days off to deal with stress.

26% — 26% of Baby Boomers take unplanned days off to deal with stress.

20% — 20% of employees said their companies enable good work/life balance.

27% — 27% of employees said their companies provide generous vacation policies.

Q1. What symptoms of stress do you experience?
Q2. Do you have any tips for handling stressful situations?

Blowing Off Steam

7. Cultural Discussion Questions

Read the passage and talk about the questions in as much detail as possible.

Dealing with Stress

For your overall wellbeing, it's important that your methods for coping with stress improve your emotional or physical health. If you feel that they are doing more harm than good, it might be time to find some healthier strategies. While unhealthy habits may temporarily mask feelings of stress, they rarely deal with the root cause and their practice could eventually lead to even more stress and anguish. For example, some people choose to overindulge in food thinking that it will give them more energy to deal with their problems, while others take out their anxiety on others by lashing out at those closest to them. A healthier approach would be to take active control of your life by learning to say "no" in order to reduce the number of tasks that you are responsible for. In addition, it is important to prioritize the importance of tasks you need to do and start every day with a clear plan for what you want to accomplish.

1. In your country, what are the most common methods for relieving stress?
2. Do you feel that your current stress management strategies are healthy? Why or why not?

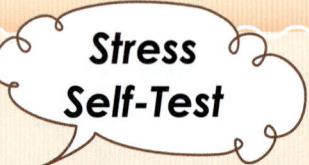

Choose a number from 1 to 4 to rate how often you are troubled by the following:

0 = Never/Rarely | 1 = Occasionally
2 = Frequently | 3 = Always/Nearly Always

#	Item	0 1 2 3	#	Item	0 1 2 3
1.	Constantly getting annoyed with people.	0 1 2 3	13.	Lack of appetite.	0 1 2 3
2.	Difficulty in making decisions.	0 1 2 3	14.	Craving for food when under pressure.	0 1 2 3
3.	Loss of sense of humor.	0 1 2 3	15.	Frequent indigestion or heartburn.	0 1 2 3
4.	Suppressed anger.	0 1 2 3	16.	Constipation or diarrhea.	0 1 2 3
5.	Difficulty concentrating.	0 1 2 3	17.	Insomnia.	0 1 2 3
6.	Inability to finish one task before rushing into another.	0 1 2 3	18.	Tendency to sweat for no good reason.	0 1 2 3
7.	Feeling you're the target of other people's animosity.	0 1 2 3	19.	Nervous twitches, nail biting, etc.	0 1 2 3
8.	Feeling unable to cope.	0 1 2 3	20.	Headaches.	0 1 2 3
9.	Wanting to cry about small problems	0 1 2 3	21.	Cramps and muscle spasms.	0 1 2 3
10.	Not interested in doing things after coming home from work.	0 1 2 3	22.	Nausea.	0 1 2 3
11.	Waking up and feeling tired after an early night.	0 1 2 3	23.	Breathlessness without exertion.	0 1 2 3
12.	Constant tiredness.	0 1 2 3	24.	Fainting spells.	0 1 2 3

- Total score between 0-25 (Few symptoms of stress)
- Total score between 26-52 (Moderate stress)
- Total score between 53-78 (Very high stress)

Q1. What were your results?
Q2. Do you feel like the test is accurate?

8. If You Ask Me

Read the discussion topic and select the statement that you believe in the most. Then role-play the scenario.

Expressing or Hiding Feelings

Stacey and Rachel are sisters who have very different personalities. Stacey is very outgoing, loves being around people, and is very honest with her opinions and her feelings. If you make her angry, she tends to explode and she expresses very clearly that you have made her angry. Various friends have commented that, while they enjoy her forthrightness, she can say and do very hurtful things when she is angry. Rachel, on the other hand, is very quiet and reserved, and she does not like drawing attention to herself. She also prefers to keep the peace and will often hide how she is really feeling. However, she usually expresses her anger and frustration to her trusted friends who are not involved, and she can sometimes hold onto a grudge or resentment for longer than her sister.

Topic Question
When dealing with anger, do you prefer to be completely honest and open or would you rather hide how you really feel for the sake of maintaining peace?

Supportive Opinion **VS** Non-Supportive Opinion

Role-play

Act out the role-play using the slang and idioms and useful expressions.

Situation
Your life is very stressful right now. You have been tasked with coordinating a huge project with an overseas branch office and due to the time differences you feel that you are on call round-the-clock dealing with questions and coordinating details from both sides. It's not uncommon for you to think you have finished all your work and then receive a pressing phone call from overseas right as you walk out the door. You feel like it is never-ending. Tonight you are having dinner with a friend and the subject of work comes up. Tell your friend about everything that is happening in your life.

Role A
- Describe your problems to your friend.
- Explain how the situation has made you feel.

Role B
- Sympathize about your friend's difficulties.
- Suggest a method for dealing with the stress.

Wrapping Up!

Tell four things that you learned from this lesson and review.

1	2	3	4

06 It Truly is a Small World

Learning Objective
Upon completion of this lesson, you will be able to **discuss the positive and negative aspects of an increasingly globalized society.**

Expression Check
- ☑ There's a real push these days for our country to be more globalized.
- ☑ We're really part of one global village.
- ☑ As the world becomes more globalized, foreign language skills are growing more important.

1. Warm Up Activity
Talk about the questions.

1. What images come to mind when you hear the word "globalization"?
2. How do you feel that globalization has changed life in your country?
3. In your opinion, what are the good and bad points of globalization?

2. Useful Phrases
Match the phrases (a-d) to the phrases (1-4) to form a complete sentence. The useful phrases are italicized.

A. *As the world becomes more globalized,*

B. *There's a real push these days for*

C. *I feel that these days we're all really*

D. Most of our customer service

1. just part of one global village.
2. foreign language skills are growing more important.
3. has been outsourced to other countries.
4. our country to become more globalized.

3. Slang & Idioms

Check out the slang and idioms and try to make your own sentences.

A	**global village** : a concept considering the world to be a single community linked by telecommunications	Tourism is one of those ways in which we become a global village.
B	**become a worldwide phenomenon** : to spread quickly globally	The rise in inflation that we are experiencing today has become a worldwide phenomenon.
C	**butterfly effect** : the idea that a very small action can cause a chain of events that has large implications	It's the butterfly effect. One magical bullet at the right place and right time can change the world.
D	**glocal** : something that is both global and local	The message of the artist's exhibition is designed to appeal to a glocal audience.

4. Key Conversation

🎧 Read through the dialogue and practice with a partner.

What a Small World

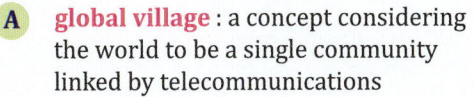

Hiro: Ah, Steve. Welcome back to Japan. It's good to see you again.

Steve: It's good to see you as well, my friend. Tell me, how have things been going with the new branch?

Hiro: As you know, there's a huge push these days for our country to become more globalized, and our company being introduced here is no exception.

Steve: The same could be said for America. When I was a kid, we could only find American restaurants. But now? Food from all over the world is available everywhere.

Hiro: You'll find the same here. McDonald's and Starbucks are everywhere. English academies are becoming more common here than anything else.

Steve: It's like we have become one global village. Just think. The more globalized we become, the less need we'll have for local languages.

Hiro: I don't know about that. There's a lot of ideas that can't be expressed in your language.

Steve: That's true. But between the Internet and the mass media, it won't be long before we feel the effects of what's happening on the other side of the world.

Hiro: We're already there, Steve. Just by sitting here talking to each other, we're proving how small the world really is.

Questions
1. Do you think this is the first time Steve and Hiro have met?
2. Do you think Steve and Hiro like the idea of globalization?

It Truly is a Small World

5. Situational Collocations

Complete the sentences using the collocations from the word box.

Word Box

- impose our standards
- vital benefits
- much-needed support
- allocation of resources
- emerging market economies
- what is at stake
- competitive pressure
- unprecedented feat

1. Succeeding in the notoriously closed-off market was an _____.
2. The corporate office will provide _____ during the months following the merger.
3. We need to carefully think about _____ before making a decision.
4. Allowing foreign businesses to enter will add _____ to the domestic market.
5. Removing import quotas will affect market behavior and shift the _____.
6. In an increasingly globalized society, we should be careful not to _____ on other cultures.
7. There are several _____ to global expansion.
8. _____ have a huge influence on the global market.

16,000 LOCATIONS across the globe, including stores in Africa, Thailand, Hong Kong, Saudi Arabia, and Elsewhere.

ONE-THIRD of Starbucks locations are outside of the US

Q. What other factors do you think might have contributed to Starbucks's global success?

It's Not Just Coffee – It's "Gourmet"

People no longer just drink coffee for its caffeine content. It's quickly become a lifestyle. Those who take their caffeine habit seriously will tell you, "It's not just coffee; it's gourmet." One company that has drastically changed views about coffee around the globe is Starbucks. Taking its name from a Moby Dick character, Starbucks has grown from a single shop in Seattle into one of the most recognizable brands in the world.

In 2018, there were nearly 30,000 Starbucks stores in 76 countries around the world.

The total number of Starbucks stores worldwide almost doubled in the decade between 2008 and 2018.

The factor that separates successful companies like Starbucks is how they approach global expansion. The big difference between the two is that while some companies may view the states in the US as many different markets, **Starbucks views the US as one large market** that is part of a whole global landscape. The **community that Starbucks has created is not just national, but global.**

6. What Would You Do?

Read the situation and explain what you would do in that situation.

Playing Tour Guide

Your company has merged with a foreign company recently in order to become more competitive in the global market. As part of the negotiation between the two companies, your employer has assigned you the role of tour guide for some representatives visiting your country from the other company. Your employer has assured you that all expenses will be covered by the company, as this merger is very important.

Q1. Where would you take your visitors? Why?

Q2. What would you feed your visitors?

Q3. How can you ensure that you make a good impression on the foreign visitors?

Levels of Globalization

Globalization most often refers to the increasing degree of connection between various countries and their economies. However, another definition involves the efforts of businesses to expand their operations into foreign markets.

According to Sales and Marketing Management magazine, businesses generally operate at one of four basic levels of globalization.

Global Company	This type of business views the world as a single market, develops an overall strategy for its various operations around the world, and applies the lessons of each country to ensure its global success.
Transnational Company	At this level, the company consists of loosely integrated business units in several countries and makes a greater effort to address the local needs of operations in each country.
International Company	At this level, the company maintains a headquarters in one country and operates branches in other countries. The company is likely to impose its home country bias on other markets rather than making a true effort to integrate into the global economy.
Multi-domestic Company	At this level, the business consists of several independent units that operate in different countries, with little communication between them.

Q. Which level of globalization does your company operate at? Explain.

It Truly is a Small World

7. Cultural Discussion Questions

Read the passage and talk about the questions in as much detail as possible.

The Global Village

If the world was a village of **100** people, **50** would be male and **50** would be female. There would be **26** children and **74** adults, **8** of whom would be over **65** years old. There would be **60** Asians, **15** Africans, **14** from the Americas, and **11** Europeans. **83** would be able to read and write, and of those, **7** would possess a university degree. **22** would own or share a computer. **77** would have a home to shelter them, and **23** would be homeless. **1** would be dying of starvation, and **15** would be malnourished, while **21** would be overweight. **87** would have access to clean drinking water.

1. How do you feel about these statistics?

2. How can we help to increase the number of people who have homes, enough food and education, and clean drinking water?

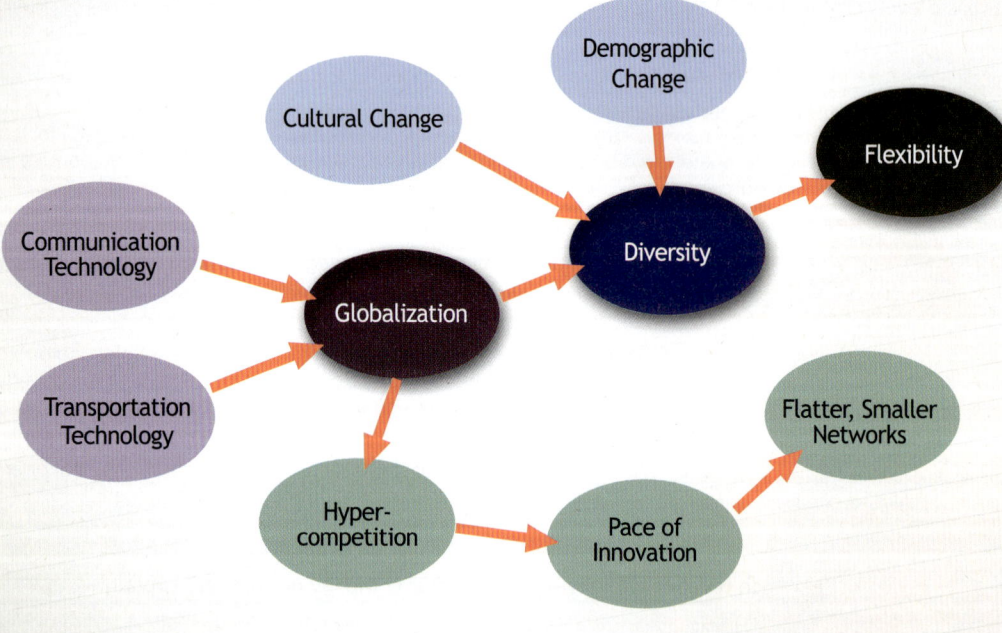

The Effect of Global Trends

In just the first two decades of the 21st century, the way that companies do business has changed more drastically than it has in the thousands of years of human history that preceded it.

Q. What are some problems or barriers associated with globalization?

8. If You Ask Me

Read the discussion topic and select the statement that you believe in the most. Then role-play the scenario.

Global Language vs. Local Language

With the world becoming increasingly globalized, the demand for a global language has also increased. As such, an entire industry of language instruction has emerged in recent years. In addition to this, entire regions of the world speak a common language, such as Spanish and Portuguese in Latin America, French in Northwestern Africa, and Chinese in much of Southeast Asia. There are definite benefits for communication in having a global language, but there are also limits. For one, the expressions and beauty of other languages are lost as the global language is embraced. Some fear that even cultural values possessed by the speakers of these languages are also at risk of being lost as their own languages become forgotten.

Topic Question

Should the world adopt a global language, or should individual cultures fight harder to preserve their unique languages?

Supportive Opinion **VS** Non-Supportive Opinion

Role-play

Act out the role-play using the slang and idioms and useful expressions.

Situation

You are currently participating in a cross-cultural training seminar at your company. The instructor has asked everyone to make a presentation about an assigned topic with a partner. You were asked to speak about the effects of globalization on your country. You want to present the benefits that you have observed, such as a wider variety of foreign foods, access to imported goods, and the ability to interact with people from around the world. Your partner, however, is very negative about the topic. He or she believes that globalization is killing your local culture and has led to many domestic jobs being outsourced overseas. Debate the pros and cons of globalization to decide which approach to take with your presentation.

Role A
- Explain your reasons for supporting globalization.
- Encourage your partner to make a positive presentation.

Role B
- Argue your case for opposing globalization.
- Try to persuade your partner to your side.

Wrapping Up!

Tell four things that you learned from this lesson and review.

1	2	3	4

07 The Dangers of Discrimination

Learning Objective

Upon completion of this lesson, you will be able to **discuss various forms of discrimination that are present in modern society.**

Expression Check

- ☑ It's so obvious that there's a glass ceiling at this company.
- ☑ People from that part of town are treated like second-class citizens.
- ☑ That comment was borderline sexual harassment.

1. Warm Up Activity

Talk about the questions.

1. There are many forms of discrimination based on factors such as gender, race, religion, sexual orientation, and socio-economic status. Which do you think is the biggest issue in your country?
2. Have you ever experienced or witnessed a form of discrimination? What happened?
3. Why do you think people discriminate against others who are different from them?

2. Useful Phrases

Match the phrases (a-d) to the phrases (1-4) to form a complete sentence. The useful phrases are italicized.

A *It's obvious that*

B *People from that part of town*

C *That comment*

D *People wrote him off as*

1 was borderline sexual harassment.

2 *there's a glass ceiling* at this company.

3 another hopeless case.

4 are *treated like second-class citizens*.

Lesson 07 / The Dangers of Discrimination

3. Slang & Idioms

Check out the slang and idioms and try to make your own sentences.

A	**racial slur**: a negative term used to refer to a particular race of people	Prosecutors hid the fact that one of their investigators used a racial slur to describe the accused.
B	**politically correct**: extremely careful not to offend or upset any group of people in society who have a disadvantage	He gave a speech that was arrogant, patronizing, and cringingly politically correct.
C	**the wrong side of the tracks**: a part of a town that is considered poor and dangerous	It's an American story about a kid who, you know, grew up on the wrong side of the tracks.
D	**stick out like a sore thumb**: be obviously different from the surrounding people or things	Diane sticks out like a sore thumb on her all-male team.

4. Key Conversation

 Read through the dialogue and practice with a partner.

That's Not Terribly PC

Molly — Hmm, what's that story about that you're reading? That guy wearing the do-rag looks kind of familiar.

Alfred — That's because he's the owner of that mega men's clothing store around the corner. Haven't you seen his face plastered all over the billboards around here lately?

Molly — You mean the ones that stick out like a sore thumb with their tacky slogans? I guess something he's doing is working, though—heard he's making a pretty penny.

Alfred — Sure is. He's from the wrong side of the tracks, and people from that part of town are pretty much treated like second-class citizens.

Molly — It just surprises me, and I know it's not terribly PC (politically correct), but I wish he'd invaded another neighborhood. That store's an eyesore compared to the upscale shops.

Alfred — So what exactly have you got against this guy, anyway?

Molly — I just don't want to see this area start to go downhill. You know the kind of people that place is going to attract.

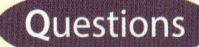

1. Do you think Molly has something against people from different backgrounds? Why or why not?
2. How do you think Alfred feels about the news story and Molly's reaction?

The Dangers of Discrimination

5. Situational Collocations

Complete the sentences using the collocations from the word box.

Word Box

- narrow-minded view
- hit a nerve
- reverse discrimination
- belittling remarks
- misogynist attitude
- public sentiment
- clear bias
- raise awareness

1. _____ can increase racism rather than working to decrease it.
2. The attempts to whip up _____ against minorities have, however, fallen flat.
3. I'm tired of putting up with his _____. I'm going to file a complaint.
4. She rapped lyrics and rhymes that addressed the _____ of her male peers.
5. The speech has really _____ with a diverse audience from all walks of life.
6. I think this is a _____, with all due respect, that you are holding.
7. The group plans to _____ of the issue with a new advertising campaign.
8. Even today, there still exists a _____ against the group.

5 FACTS About Pregnant Women in the Workplace

A survey conducted with **357,500** working women with a child under two revealed **18.8**% faced discrimination in the workplace and **29.3**% left the workforce permanently while pregnant or after having their child.

The survey showed **31,200** women felt they received negative comments from their manager or colleagues, **22,900** said they missed out on a promotion, and **10,100** reported their duties were changed without consultation.

 17.4% of women took 14 to 26 weeks of paid leave from work.

 18.8% of pregnant women reported experiencing discrimination in the workplace.

 29.3% of women leave the workforce permanently before or after the birth of their child.

 7,800 of women surveyed wanted better flexible working arrangements.

five 42.8% of mothers returning to work state grandparents are the preferred method of childcare.

Q1. Is it common for women to quit working to raise children in your country?

Q2. In your opinion, do you feel the benefits of a double income are worth a woman missing out on important moments in her child's life?

Lesson 07 / The Dangers of Discrimination

6. What Would You Do?

Read the situation and explain what you would do in that situation.

Age Discrimination in the Workplace

You have been working with a senior staff member for about three months now, and you have become increasingly uncomfortable around him. He often asks you to do petty tasks and personal errands that really are not your responsibility. You feel he is abusing his rank and power for personal benefits. He is older than you, and he obviously believes he deserves extra respect because you are his junior.

Q1. Would it be better to talk to him directly or should you go through HR?

Q2. What would you say to him to let him know his actions are unacceptable?

Q3. Is this kind of problem common in your country's corporate environment?

Social Class Discrimination

Defining social classes is a controversial issue, with countless definitions, models, and even disputes over the validity of the boundaries that the process requires. Below you will find a simple model, which divides people into three groups: "rich", "middle class", and "poor."

Q1. Do you think categorizing people into social classes is useful? Why or why not?

Q2. What do you think the traits of the three groups might be?

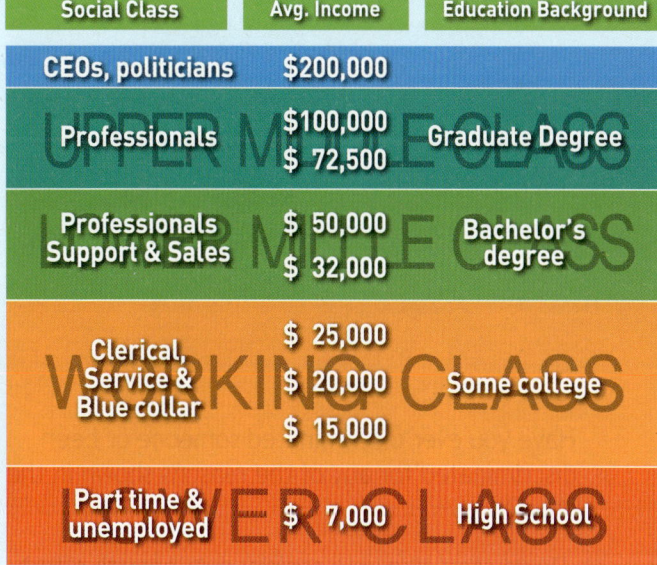

Social Class	Avg. Income	Education Background
CEOs, politicians	$200,000	
Professionals	$100,000 / $72,500	Graduate Degree
Professionals / Support & Sales	$50,000 / $32,000	Bachelor's degree
Clerical, Service & Blue collar	$25,000 / $20,000 / $15,000	Some college
Part time & unemployed	$7,000	High School

(UPPER CLASS / UPPER MIDDLE CLASS / LOWER MIDDLE CLASS / WORKING CLASS / LOWER CLASS)

The Dangers of Discrimination

7. Cultural Discussion Questions

Read the passage and talk about the questions in as much detail as possible.

Gender Discrimination in the Workplace

The status of men and women varies widely from country to country. Women have gained equal rights in many countries. However, this does not always translate into equal treatment or opportunities. Men may face discrimination as they pursue what are considered traditionally "female" occupations or become stay-at-home dads. In the workplace, there may be unspoken expectations for each gender and limits set upon the advancement of women. They may be discriminated against because they are not expected to be able to do a job as effectively as the opposite gender.

1. Do men and women have equal opportunities for employment and advancement in your country?
2. Do you feel that your workplace places different expectations on each sex? Why or why not?
3. Share an example of someone in your country who was able to successfully push through the glass ceiling.

Do You Feel Discriminated Against?

A recent survey asked 343,000 people to tell about reasons why they had felt discriminated against in the past. the chart on the right shows the results.

Respondents Who Felt Discriminated Against by Reason

Reason	Percent
Skin color, race, ethnicity, or nationality	~55
Dress or appearance	~20
Age	~17
Gender	~15
Occupation	~14
The language they speak	~11
Religious beliefs	~9
Disability or health issue	~8
Marital status	~5
Political position	~4
Family status	~4

Percent of those discriminated against who selected this reason

Q1. Have you ever discriminated someone or been discriminated for any of the reasons shown in the chart?

Q2. Do you feel like your society puts enough effort into reducing social discrimination in your country? Why or why not?

Lesson 07 / The Dangers of Discrimination

8. If You Ask Me

Read the discussion topic and select the statement that you believe in the most. Then role-play the scenario.

Gay Rights

In the US, equal treatment and equal rights for gay and lesbian individuals has been a hot issue in the realm of politics, and everyone seems to have an opinion. Laws are changing in some states, opening the way for legal marriage for couples of the same gender. Some people strongly support the right of people to marry and have legal equality regardless of sexual orientation. Others firmly defend traditional concepts of marriage and reject the idea.

Topic Question

Are people in same-sex partnerships entitled to the same rights as those in traditional relationships?

Supportive Opinion VS **Non-Supportive Opinion**

Role-play

Act out the role-play using the slang and idioms and useful expressions.

Situation

You are having coffee with a friend when he or she mentions that you seem upset. Recently you applied for a promotion at work and were turned down in favor of someone who is younger and less qualified. You feel strongly that your boss discriminated against you because of a specific reason (age, sex, appearance, etc.). In the past, your boss has always promoted people from a certain background. You feel that you have enough evidence to file a complaint against your boss but you are scared that coming forward could have some repercussions.

Role A
- Tell your partner about the incident and how it made you feel.
- Ask for your partner's advice on how to deal with the problem.

Role B
- Sympathize with your partner about the unfairness of his or her situation.
- Encourage your partner to visit HR to file a complaint.

Wrapping Up! Tell four things that you learned from this lesson and review.

1   2   3   4

08 Flattery Will Get You Nowhere

Learning Objective

Upon completion of this lesson, you will be able to **offer and respond to flattery in personal and professional situations.**

Expression Check

☑ I love that tie you're wearing. It really brings out your eyes.
☑ You handled that like the true professional you are.
☑ You do wonders for my ego.

1. Warm Up Activity

Talk about the questions.

1. Have you ever tried to gain favor with someone by using flattery?
2. How do you feel when someone flatters you?
3. How often do you compliment people? What types of compliments do you pay the most often?

2. Useful Phrases

Match the phrases (a-d) to the phrases (1-4) to form a complete sentence. The useful phrases are italicized.

A *She complimented me*

B *He seemed unaware of*

C *You're much too intelligent to*

D Mary told me that my hair looked nice,

1 the girl's *fawning admiration*.

2 so I *returned her compliment*.

3 *on* my new tie.

4 *fall for his flattery*.

3. Slang & Idioms

Check out the slang and idioms and try to make your own sentences.

A	**fish for a compliment** : try to make someone say something nice about you, usually by first criticizing yourself	Tara's always fishing for compliments by talking about how she couldn't get her hair the way she wanted it.
B	**backhanded compliments** : a remark which seems to be a compliment but could also be understood as an insult	He's always offending people with his backhanded compliments.
C	**butter someone up** : praise or flatter someone in order to make him or her more receptive or willing	Percy was always buttering up the boss, so he was surprised when he failed to get a promotion.
D	**apple-polish** : someone who utilizes gifts and flattery as a means of gaining favor	Mr. Green tries to apple-polish his supervisor.

4. Key Conversation

Read through the dialogue and practice with a partner.

Flattery Could Get You In Trouble

Paula Mom! Susie's doing everything I do. Make her stop.

Mrs. Wilson Don't be cross with her. "Imitation is the sincerest form of flattery." She just wants to be like her big sister. She'll soon grow out of it.

Paula That's not flattery — that's just a backhanded compliment.

Mrs. Wilson Well just don't listen to her. I told you, Susie will soon grow up. She's not that much younger than you are.

Paula I hope it doesn't take too long, She's driving me crazy!

Mrs. Wilson Keep thinking about what I told you. Imitation is the sincerest form of flattery.

Paula OK, OK. Hey, Mom. You remember Mary, that girl in my class, don't you? She's always trying to copy me, too!

Mrs. Wilson You must be a very popular girl if others in your class are beginning to copy you. You must feel flattered!

Paula Imitation may be the sincerest form of flattery, but I don't feel very flattered when Mary copies my answers to the homework.

Mrs. Wilson Oh dear, I guess that kind of "flattery" could get you in trouble at school!

Questions
1. Do you think Mrs. Wilson's advice to Paula is good?
2. What advice would you give Paula about Mary?

Flattery Will Get You Nowhere

5. Situational Collocations

Complete the sentences using the collocations from the word box.

Word Box

- a genuine compliment
- from the heart
- lavish him with compliments
- sincere admiration
- an obvious suck-up
- hidden agenda
- rubs me the wrong way
- thinly veiled criticism

1. He's such _____. I couldn't believe what he said to Mr. Johnson.
2. Everyone understood immediately that the compliment was nothing more than a _____.
3. She spoke about her _____ for the work we had done.
4. When is somebody going to come clean and reveal the real _____?
5. Something about the sound of his voice _____.
6. I was surprised when he offered me _____.
7. Always speak _____ and your sincerity will be obvious.
8. Everyone was doing their best to _____.

With the Boss, It Had Better Be Good...

Flattery is an incredibly common way to win influence, but is it always the best strategy to impress your boss? Experts say no.

Successful flattery takes skill. Everyone wants to win his or her supervisor's approval and admiration, which means that flattery can sometimes come across as insincere and desperate. Although you might think a kind remark will win you favor, research shows that empty compliments can backfire and have the opposite effect.

Flattery is one form of impression management. Another example in the workplace would be displaying initiative and dedication to your work. The choice of whether or not to attempt these strategies largely depends on the type of organization and situation. However, the general consensus from experts is it is best to err on the side of caution when flattering your boss.

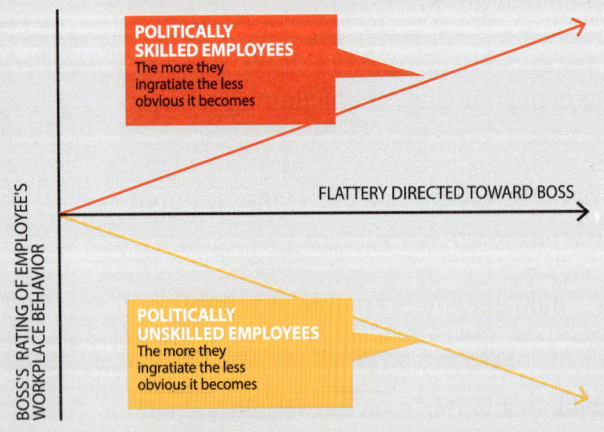

BOSS'S RATING OF EMPLOYEE'S WORKPLACE BEHAVIOR

POLITICALLY SKILLED EMPLOYEES
The more they ingratiate the less obvious it becomes

FLATTERY DIRECTED TOWARD BOSS

POLITICALLY UNSKILLED EMPLOYEES
The more they ingratiate the less obvious it becomes

Q. Have you ever attempted to flatter your boss? What did you say? Did it have the desired effect?

6. What Would You Do?

Read the situation and explain what you would do in that situation.

A White Lie

Your spouse just got a new haircut and is fishing for a compliment. However, you do not like the hairstyle at all and feel that it is not flattering. You are in a predicament because you want to please your spouse but you also made a promise when you got married to always be honest with one another. Your spouse is very sensitive and will be hurt if you tell the trust. At the same time, you feel that the truth may help them avoid making similar mistakes at the salon in the future.

Q1. Will you tell a white lie or tell the truth?

Q2. What could you say to make the truth less hurtful?

Q3. Do you think it is important to always be honest with people you love? Why or why not?

How Does Your Blood Type Respond to Flattery?

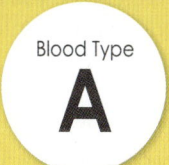

Flattery does not work for Blood Type A as they do not trust others easily.

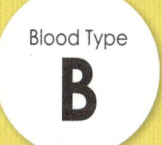

Blood Type B loves to hear good things about himself. Flattery definitely works.

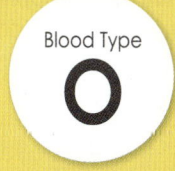

Flattery works well for Blood Type O. However, try to get close to them before trying it.

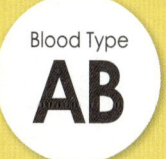

Flattery has a reverse effect on composed and calm Blood Type AB. It might cause hatred.

Q. What's your blood type? Do you feel like the generalization above is accurate in your case?

7. Cultural Discussion Questions

Read the passage and talk about the questions in as much detail as possible.

Good Intentions, Bad Results

Complimenting someone you don't know well can be like walking in a minefield. You never know when your words could set off an unintended reaction. There are many factors to consider when attempting to flatter someone. In some cultures, it is considered better to be humble and politely deny a compliment. In some cases, a compliment could make a shy person uncomfortable. It is also important to pay careful attention to the wording. Occasionally compliments can be interpreted in different ways. For example, "That dress is nicer than the one you wore yesterday," might be understood to imply that your fashion choices yesterday were questionable. In addition, statements like "You handled that situation much better than John," could bring out feelings of competitiveness or superiority.

1. Is it expected to praise someone for work they have done in your country?
2. What is the appropriate way to respond to a compliment in your culture?

Are You Better Than Your Boss?

Flattering your boss doesn't always mean that you think your boss is great. Do you think everyone butters up the boss because he or she is so brilliant? A recent survey gives us surprising insight into what people actually think of their superiors.

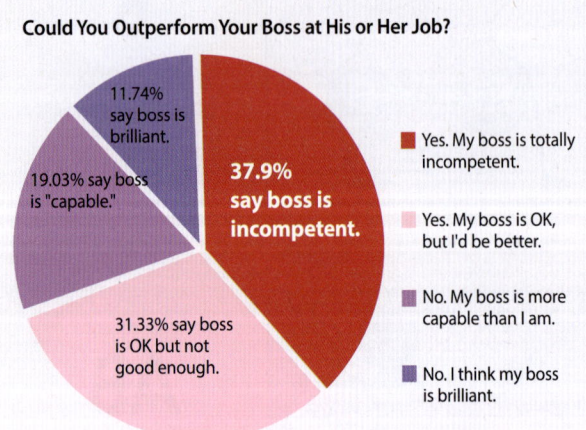

Could You Outperform Your Boss at His or Her Job?

- 11.74% say boss is brilliant.
- 19.03% say boss is "capable."
- 37.9% say boss is incompetent.
- 31.33% say boss is OK but not good enough.

■ Yes. My boss is totally incompetent.
■ Yes. My boss is OK, but I'd be better.
■ No. My boss is more capable than I am.
■ No. I think my boss is brilliant.

In the US, 69.23% of 3,023 respondents stated that they could outperform their boss. Less than 12% of them think their boss is actually "brilliant".

On the contrary, results from Asian countries yielded slightly different results with only 61.3% believing that they are capable of doing a better job. In fact, a relatively whopping 18.4% believe their boss is brilliant.

Q. Why do you think the responses from the two cultures were so different?

8. If You Ask Me

Read the discussion topic and select the statement that you believe in the most. Then role-play the scenario.

The Buttered Boss

A managerial position will soon be opening up at your company and rumor has it the position will be filled internally. This has caused quite a stir in your department as several people are equally qualified for the job. However, you have recently noticed one person trying to butter up the boss. You know it is disingenuine because just a few weeks ago that same person had nothing good to say about him. Although you don't want to believe this strategy could work, you notice that the potential candidate has been given several tasks lately that are above his level of responsibility. As much as it pains you to think that your boss has succumbed to blatant flattery, it seems like your co-worker is being tested for the position.

Topic Question

Would you keep quiet about the situation or would you try to talk to your boss about your suspicions?

Supportive Opinion VS **Non-Supportive Opinion**

Role-play

Act out the role-play using the slang and idioms and useful expressions.

Situation

You are the supervisor of a small department. Recently one of the people under you has been complimenting you endlessly. At first, you found the attention flattering, but as time goes on, it has become more and more uncomfortable. You know that other people have noticed and you realize that you need to talk to that person about the problem before the situation gets even more awkward. Find a diplomatic way to let him or her know that the compliments are too much.

Role A
- Say that you appreciate his or her kind words.
- Explain how you feel about the constant flattery.

Role B
- Apologize for making your supervisor uncomfortable.
- Insist that you only had good intentions.

Tell four things that you learned from this lesson and review.

1	2	3	4

09 Dealing With Conflict

Learning Objective
Upon completion of this lesson, you will be able to **discuss different methods for dealing with conflict.**

Expression Check
- ☑ I tend to avoid conflict at all costs.
- ☑ I prefer to take the bull by the horns.
- ☑ Let's just agree to disagree.

1. Warm Up Activity
Talk about the questions.

1. When you see the word "conflict," what do you think of?
2. What are some different ways you know of for dealing with a conflict?
3. Do you tend to avoid conflict, or would you rather deal with it directly?

2. Useful Phrases
Match the phrases (a-d) to the phrases (1-4) to form a complete sentence. The useful phrases are italicized.

A. I don't think there's *a clear right or wrong answer*, so

B. I don't like arguing.

C. I feel like such a *pushover* sometimes.

D. If *you're stuck* and don't know what to do,

1. I'm always *giving into other people's demands*.

2. *let's just agree to disagree.*

3. just *attack the problem head-on.*

4. I *tend to avoid conflict at all costs.*

3. Slang & Idioms

Check out the slang and idioms and try to make your own sentences.

A	**let sleeping dogs lie** : avoid interfering in a situation that is currently causing no problems	*We know that we will never reach an agreement on this matter, so it's better to let sleeping dogs lie.*
B	**battle of wills** : a conflict, argument or struggle where both sides are determined to win at all costs	*Annie and Phil were engaged in a silent battle of wills, each refusing to leave.*
C	**pushover** : a person who is easy to overcome or influence	*He's a tough negotiator - you won't find him a pushover.*
D	**take the bull by the horns** : deal directly and decisively with a difficult, dangerous, or unpleasant situation	*It's time to take the bull by the horns and get this job done.*

4. Key Conversation

🎧 Read through the dialogue and practice with a partner.

Agree to Disagree

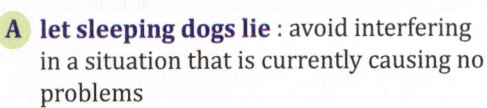

Mother	Lisa. Come here, have a seat and tell me how you are doing today.
Lisa	Well, Mom, I'm doing all right, I guess. My boyfriend is being an idiot again.
Mother	Oh, a rough patch in your relationship, then?
Lisa	Something like that. He makes me so angry sometimes!
Mother	What did he do this time?
Lisa	That's just the point! He never does anything! I always ask him what's wrong and he just says that he's fine, but I know that's not true. His dad is being way too hard on him, and he's been having issues at work. Whenever I try to press further, he just gets upset and walks out the door rather than discussing things.
Mother	Sounds to me like he tends to avoid conflict at all costs.
Lisa	Yeah, tell me about it! Me, I prefer to take the bull by the horns. Nothing ever gets solved by just walking away.
Mother	I don't know about that. Sometimes walking away is the best thing you can do.
Lisa	Let's just agree to disagree on that one, OK?

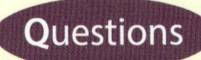

1. Do you think Lisa understands her boyfriend?
2. Do you think that Lisa's mother shares her views on dealing with conflict?

Dealing With Conflict

Is Conflict Always Bad?

For most of us, dealing with conflict demands lots of energy and creates stress. Sometimes, it makes for a generally unpleasant experience. Our belief that conflict is always negative and unpleasant can lead us to avoid issues or delay discussions. However, we need to look at the possible positive payoffs of conflict. Read the following quotes and consider the question at the end.

"Whenever you're in conflict with someone, there's one factor that can make the difference between damaging your relationship and deepening it. That factor is attitude." **by William James**

"Remember not only to say the right thing in the right place, but far more difficult still, to leave unsaid the wrong thing at the tempting moment." **by Benjamin Franklin**

"Conflicts may be the sources of defeat, lost life and a limitation of our potentiality, but they may also lead to greater depth of living and the birth of more far-reaching unities, which flourish in the tensions that engender them." **by Karl Jaspers**

"In critical and baffling situations, it's always best to return to first principle and simple action." **by Sir Winston S. Churchill**

Q Do you think conflict is always a negative thing? Why? Back up your opinion with evidence from your personal experience.

5. Situational Collocations

Complete the sentences using the collocations from the word box.

Word Box

| · butting heads | · awkward silence | · a shouting match | · disrespectful attitude |
| · make a case for | · a low blow | · seething with rage | · stubborn pride |

① He understood that it would be foolish to end a lifelong friendship for _____.

② Finally, after a few seconds of _____, Jack finally spoke.

③ Of course, being a witty individual, you aren't going to resort to such _____.

④ Earlier this week, protestors got into _____ with the police.

⑤ He can be cocky and arrogant, always _____ with his co-workers.

⑥ Some residents sought to _____ enforcing parking regulations in their overcrowded neighborhood.

⑦ The brash and _____ of his argument made the situation worse.

⑧ Staring after him, still _____, I breathed heavily.

6. What Would You Do?

Read the situation and explain what you would do in that situation.

Problems with the Spouse

Your best friend has come to you for advice about problems with his/her spouse. Your friend is frustrated that his/her spouse always seems to be picking a fight with him/her and engaging in a battle of wills. You know that your friend is the type who prefers to let sleeping dogs lie, and he/she does not like conflict very much.

What sort of advice would you give to your friend?

Q1. What advice would you give your friend?

Q2. What do you think your friend should say to his/her spouse?

Q3. Do you think it is easy for a couple to overcome this kind of problem? Why or why not?

Conflict & Personalities

Due to individual personality traits, two people might have a very different point of view on how to handle a disagreement. This is one of the factors that can sometimes escalate small conflicts into feuds. For this reason, it is essential to take personality into consideration when evaluating how to settle a disagreement. Let's look at how to best defuse conflicts with specific personality types.

- Logical (Withhold)
- Analytical
- Practical
- Reserved (Ask)
- Assertive (Tell)
- Amiable
- Extravert
- Emotional (Display)

If you are more of a logical or practical person, you tend to analyze the conflict and try to deal with it realistically. You are more controlled than impulsive.

On the other hand, if you are more of an emotional and people-oriented person, you tend to be open and friendly to communicate more. You try to show your own feelings regardless of what is right or wrong because you put great emphasis on the value of relationships.

If you are an assertive and outgoing person, you are forthright and stubborn – holding your views strongly and refusing to back down when you express your opinions.

On the other hand, if you are a reserved person, you subscribe to the view that everyone is entitled to their opinions, even if they differ from your own. You feel no need to have the last word in driving home your particular viewpoint.

7. Cultural Discussion Questions

Read the passage and talk about the questions in as much detail as possible.

Conflict Styles

Psychologists have identified five different conflict styles. **FIGHTERS** prefer fighting every battle to win and insist on being right. **COLLABORATORS** prefer helping everyone to win and do not make a decision until everyone is happy. **COMPROMISERS** like to meet halfway on most points. **AVOIDERS** dislike conflict and would rather walk away from a fight or ignore the problem until it goes away. Finally, **ACCOMMODATORS** always try to keep the peace by accepting the other person's opinion, even if they disagree.

1. Which conflict style are you? How does it affect the way you deal with disagreements?
2. In your country, how do people usually deal with conflict?

3 Ways to Handle Disagreements Effectively

Separate Yourself from your Position

If we involve ourselves personally with our positions, we will have a harder time being objective about them. That lack of objectivity can prolong a disagreement needlessly. Try to view your position not as "your" position, but merely as "a" position. In the same way, if you have an issue with someone else's position, make clear that your concern is with the issue, not with the person.

#1

Listen

Listen to people completely, if you can, before responding. If you have to interrupt because the other person is being long-winded, try to summarize your understanding first. For example, you can say, "OK, so what I hear you saying is…" and then say in your own words what they said to be sure you are getting it right.

#2

Bring a Mediator

If you realize that someone is not listening or that you are struggling to understand what they are saying, then bring a mediator. You can simply share your troubles in communicating with each other with the mediator and then ask for an unbiased opinion about the issue you have in an effort to resolve it.

#3

8. If You Ask Me

Read the discussion topic and select the statement that you believe in the most. Then role-play the scenario.

Exploring Conflict

Although it makes many people uncomfortable, conflict is a regular part of our everyday lives. It is through conflict that friendships develop and deepen, as well as break apart. Conflict can be a catalyst for change. It is the reason that civilization has continually advanced rather than staying the same. However, conflict can sometimes have negative effects. In international situations, it can lead to war, the destruction of property, and the loss of countless lives. In our personal lives, conflict can result in a variety of problems ranging from lost relationships to a lot of hurt feelings.

Topic Question

Do you think that conflict should mostly be seen as a positive thing (supportive), or is it a decidedly negative influence (non-supportive)?

Supportive Opinion VS **Non-Supportive Opinion**

Role-play

Act out the role-play using the slang and idioms and useful expressions.

Situation

You and your partner are working together on a team project at work. You notice that your partner has been missing a lot of team meetings lately. After all the hard work is done, he or she shows up at the last minute with a flimsy excuse. You have had a similar problem with him or her in the past. You want to confront your co-worker about the issue, but you are worried about stirring up conflict in your workplace. Decide the best way to approach the situation and take the bull by the horns.

Role A
- Ask your co-worker to talk.
- Explain the problem and how his or her actions are affecting others.

Role B
- Apologize for your behavior.
- Promise to be better in the future.

Wrapping Up!

Tell four things that you learned from this lesson and review.

1.
2.
3.
4.

10 A Lost Passport

Learning Objective
Upon completion of this lesson, you will be able to **cope with losing personal identification in a foreign country.**

Expression Check
- ☑ I'm pretty sure I packed my passport, but I can't find it anywhere.
- ☑ How am I supposed to drive when I misplaced my license?
- ☑ Do you remember me putting my credit card back in my wallet?

1. Warm Up Activity
Talk about the questions.

1. Have you ever lost your passport or another important form of ID?
2. Do you use your passport or another form of ID when traveling domestically?
3. What forms of ID do you usually carry with you on an average day?

2. Useful Phrases
Match the phrases (a-d) to the phrases (1-4) to form a complete sentence. The useful phrases are italicized.

A *I'm pretty sure* I packed my passport,

B *How am I supposed to*

C *Do you remember me*

D Oh no! *What did I do with*

1 putting my credit card back into my wallet?

2 drive when I misplaced my license?

3 my ID?

4 but *I can't find it anywhere.*

3. Slang & Idioms

Check out the slang and idioms and try to make your own sentences.

A cross that bridge when I come to it : deal with a problem when and if it arises

It's hard to say now. I guess I'm just going to have to cross that bridge when I come to it.

B rocky road : have difficulties or problems to deal with

He knew he had a long rocky road ahead of him if he wanted to become a doctor.

C Green Card : an ID card carried by a permanent resident of the US

This line is for citizens and Green Card holders only.

D government issued ID : any official document which may be used to prove a person's identity

Don't forget to bring a government issued ID or you won't be allowed on your flight.

4. Key Conversation

Read through the dialogue and practice with a partner.

Let Me See Some Identification

Graham Could I see some ID and your boarding pass, ma'am?

Sarah Well, here's my boarding pass. I'm sorry, but I can't seem to find my passport anywhere. I'm pretty sure I packed it.

Graham I'm sorry, ma'am, but without any ID, I can't let you past this check point.

Sarah I must have left it on the kitchen counter. I'll miss my flight if I leave to get it. Could I maybe use another form of identification?

Graham Well, since you are taking a domestic flight, you don't need your passport. Any government issued ID will be fine.

Sarah OK. Let me see. Insurance card, Visa, American Express, check card. This should just take me a minute.

Graham Do you happen to have a driver's license?

Sarah Of course! That's right! How could I have driven here without one? Here you go.

Graham Thank you, you can go through.

Questions
1. Do you think Sarah is an organized person?
2. What do you think would have happened to Sarah if this was an international flight?

A Lost Passport

What Happens to Lost Property?

Travelers annually leave millions of personally important items such as wallets, keys, passports, cell phones, and eyeglasses behind in hotels, airports, airplanes, and rental cars.

Average number of lost items recovered in airports and planes: **10,000 items / per month**

So, where does lost property end up?

Airports store items for an average of 30 to 90 days and then items are either sold, discarded, or donated to charity.

Why can't all items be returned to the owners?

✓ Lost items often do not contain an owner's contact information.

✓ They are not reported lost.

✓ Some electronic devices are locked – making it difficult to return to the owner.

Q1. Have you ever lost something while you were traveling? Were you able to get it back?

Q2. Do you usually use traveler's insurance? Why or why not?

5. Situational Collocations

Complete the sentences using the collocations from the word box.

Word Box

· report my loss · careless mistake · lose sight of
· keep track of · claim lost articles · left it behind
· seemed out of it · mild annoyance

1. What do you mean you lost it? I asked you to _____ the bag.
2. I'm sorry but I must have _____ on the table.
3. Surprisingly, few people know to go to the lost and found to _____.
4. Losing my passport was no _____.
5. If I were you, I'd _____ to the airline.
6. Don't worry. It was just a _____.
7. I'm not surprised he forgot his keys. He _____ when he left.
8. I don't know how you managed to _____ such a big suitcase.

6. What Would You Do?

Read the situation and explain what you would do in that situation.

Last-Minute Decision

In your rush to get to the airport for your return flight at the end of your vacation, you forgot to pick up your passport from the reception desk. You still have a little time before your flight, but you worry you might miss it if you return to the hotel to get it yourself. There isn't another flight out until tomorrow and you are supposed to be back at work in the morning.

Q1. What would you do in this situation?

Q2. Who could you ask for help at the hotel? What would you say?

Q3. What might happen if you miss your flight?

7. Cultural Discussion Questions

Read the passage and talk about the questions in as much detail as possible.

Tourist Visas

Many nations have reciprocal agreements allowing their citizens to make short stays in other countries without applying for a visa in advance. In these cases, travelers are allowed to enter without paying for a visa and given the opportunity to travel for a short period as tourists. In most cases, visits are limited to 90 days before additional documentation is required. When traveling abroad, it is important to check the requirements for your country's citizens to make sure that your paperwork is in order before leaving for a trip.

1. What are the most popular foreign travel destinations for people in your country? Do you need a visa to go?

2. Should all countries offer visa-free stays for tourists? What are some possible reasons for asking people to apply for visas in advance?

A Lost Passport

SMART Passport

Passports contain a variety of security features, which fall into two categories: Physical Security Features and Logical Security Features. Read more about what makes these features unique below.

Physical Security Features

There are 3 categories of Physical Security Features:

1st level – Security features seen by the naked eye, such as: ID picture, hologram, optically variable Ink (OVI), thermo-chromic inks, metallic security threads, personalized shadows, and graphic design (water marks, deformation pattern, Guilloche, intaglio, rainbow printing, etc.).

2nd level – Hidden security features authenticated by using simple devices: Magnifying glass, UV lamp, 2D barcode reader, smart card reader, special simple lenses, other electronic devices, and biometric data verification. Typical measures include Micro-text, UV and IR inks, magnetic inks, tagged inks, and toners.

3rd level – Hidden security features authenticated at forensic laboratory level using special equipment.

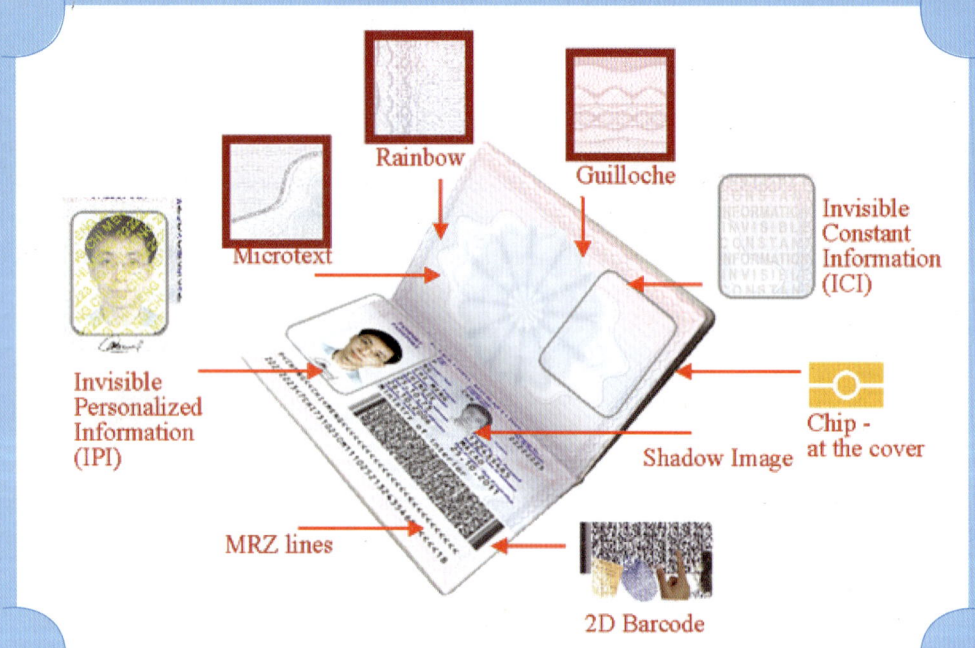

Logical Security Features

These Logical Security Features apply specifically to smart (chip-based) cards (or e-Passports), both contact and contactless smart cards which make use of highly-secured encryption features.

 Describe your country's passport. What kinds of security features does it contain?

8. If You Ask Me

Read the discussion topic and select the statement that you believe in the most. Then role-play the scenario.

To Carry or Not to Carry?

When traveling abroad, it is important to make sure that you keep track of important travel documents, such as your passport. Some people claim that the safest option is to lock important things in a room safe or to leave it with hotel security. When they go out to see the sights, they choose to just take a photocopy of their documents with them. However, other people insist that it is necessary to keep the original copies with them at all times unless there is some kind of disaster or emergency.

Topic Question

Should you leave your passport in a secure place when you travel (supportive) or is it better to keep it on you at all times (non-supportive)?

Supportive Opinion

VS

Non-Supportive Opinion

Role-play

Act out the role-play using the slang and idioms and useful expressions.

Situation

When you arrive at the airport, you discover that you don't have your passport with you. You are traveling abroad and need to show a visa to receive your ticket from the check-in counter. You are certain it is in your bedroom but you aren't sure of the exact location. You must call a family member to ask someone to find the passport and bring it to you.

Role A
- Explain the situation and tell your family member where to look.
- Ask him or her to bring it to you.

Role B
- Agree to help.
- Say you have found the passport and are on your way.

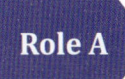

Wrapping Up! Tell four things that you learned from this lesson and review.

1   2   3   4

11 Job Satisfaction

Learning Objective

Upon completion of this lesson, you will be able to **discuss the relationship between employers and their employees.**

Expression Check

- ☑ Why do I have to wait around until the boss is ready to go home?
- ☑ I've never understood why we have to do that.
- ☑ My boss and I are finally seeing eye to eye on things.

1. Warm Up Activity

Talk about the questions.

1. Do you have a good relationship with your current manager or boss?
2. Have you ever worked for a difficult manager or boss?
3. What do you think are the characteristics of an effective manager?

2. Useful Phrases

Match the phrases (a-d) to the phrases (1-4) to form a complete sentence. The useful phrases are italicized.

A Why *do I have to wait around*	1 *seeing eye to eye* on things.
B *I've never understood*	2 until the boss is ready to go home?
C My boss and I are finally	3 *learn to respect my authority.*
D *I just wish they would*	4 *why* we have to do that.

Lesson 11 / Job Satisfaction 71

3. Slang & Idioms

Check out the slang and idioms and try to make your own sentences.

A	**pick up the slack** : do the work that someone else has stopped doing but still needs to be done	If Sue gets a job, Mike will have to pick up the slack at home.
B	**perks** : money, goods, or other benefits an employee receives	The perks are the only thing that keeps me from quitting.
C	**punch in / out** : record the time of one's arrival or departure at work	Could you punch me out? My hands are full.
D	**slave driver** : a person who works others very hard	Mr. Sampson is such a slave driver. I can't believe he asked us to stay late again.

4. Key Conversation

🎧 **Read through the dialogue and practice with a partner.**

Company Policy

Jessica	James? Are you still at work?
James	Hi, Jess. Listen, Mr. Fuji has us working another all-nighter, so I don't think I'll be able to make it to dinner tonight. I'm sorry to cancel on you again.
Jessica	Really? Well, that's OK. I guess I'll just tell my parents you won't be able to meet them tonight either – and call the restaurant to cancel our reservation.
James	I'm really sorry about this. It's just that Mr. Fuji dropped a bomb on us earlier today and told us we have until tomorrow to finish this project he just found out about this morning.
Jessica	Well, that's kind of unfair. Doesn't Mr. Fuji understand that his employees might have lives of their own?
James	It's company policy that the whole team has to stick around until everyone finishes.
Jessica	He sounds like a slave driver to me. I mean, why should you have to stay until the boss is ready to go home?
James	I've never understood why we have to do that either, or why they don't give us more notice for these big projects. But, at least he's not like my last boss.
Jessica	Yeah, you told me about him. He lazed around, enjoying the perks of being in charge, and expected you to pick up the slack.
James	Yeah, exactly. Oh, gotta go. Mr. Fuji wants to see me.

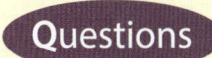 1. Do you think James enjoys his job?
2. How do you think Jessica feels about James's job?

Job Satisfaction

5. Situational Collocations

Complete the sentences using the collocations from the word box.

Word Box

- toxic work environment
- drives bottom-line results
- gives a voice to
- innate strengths
- collective bargaining power
- impact focus
- create synergy
- a clear path for

1. The CEO's open-door policy _____ all workers who have ideas to contribute.
2. I'm glad to be out of that _____.
3. You have excellent ideas to _____ in the workplace.
4. A good working environment increases innovation, builds trust and _____.
5. The process can be made significantly easier if there is _____ employees to follow.
6. The staff chose to exercise their _____ by going on strike.
7. The seminar aims to identify and exploit the workers' _____ and talents.
8. I believe that the new program will simultaneously _____ and raise morale in the workplace.

What Employees Really Want

There is obviously a disconnect between employers and employees. Employers believe that monetary compensation and promotion are the main things their employees desire. However, employees want to be appreciated, cared for, and "in" on things.

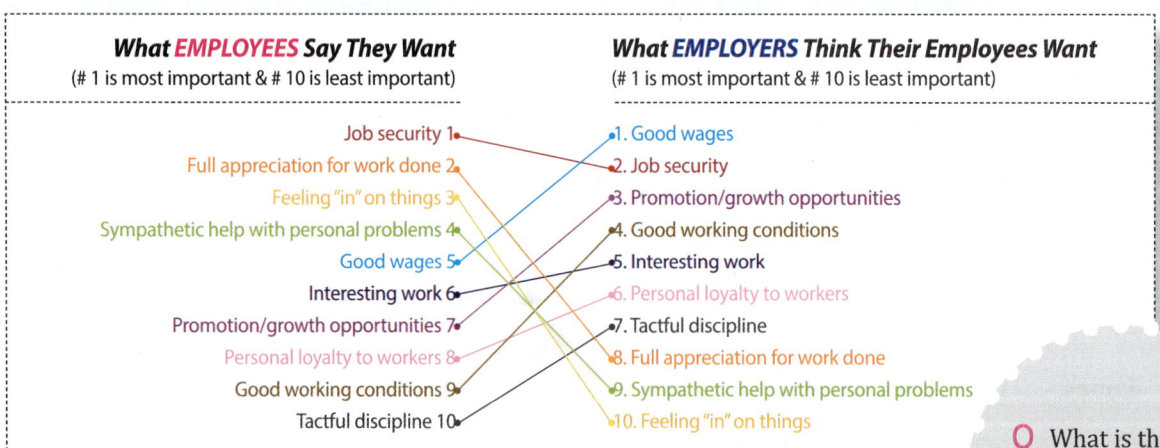

What EMPLOYEES Say They Want
(# 1 is most important & # 10 is least important)

1. Job security
2. Full appreciation for work done
3. Feeling "in" on things
4. Sympathetic help with personal problems
5. Good wages
6. Interesting work
7. Promotion/growth opportunities
8. Personal loyalty to workers
9. Good working conditions
10. Tactful discipline

What EMPLOYERS Think Their Employees Want
(# 1 is most important & # 10 is least important)

1. Good wages
2. Job security
3. Promotion/growth opportunities
4. Good working conditions
5. Interesting work
6. Personal loyalty to workers
7. Tactful discipline
8. Full appreciation for work done
9. Sympathetic help with personal problems
10. Feeling "in" on things

Q What is the number one thing that you want from your job? Why?

6. What Would You Do?

Read the situation and explain what you would do in that situation.

Burning the Midnight Oil

Your boss is continually keeping you late at the office, usually by assigning tasks with too little notice to finish them within your set working hours. Although he is also working hard alongside you, you feel that you are spending less and less time with your family lately. Your spouse and children have said that they miss you, and you have missed out on some important family events because of your hectic schedule. You feel that this lack of notice is unacceptable and you are unsure of how much longer you can continue to work under these conditions.

Q1. Would you talk to your boss directly? What could you say?

Q2. Do you think it would be better to cut your losses and find a new job?

Q3. What could you do to prioritize your relationships with family and friends?

EMPLOYER VS EMPLOYEE

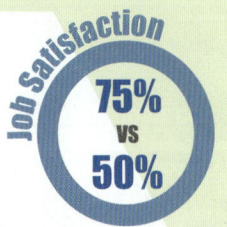

Job Satisfaction
75% vs 50%

About 75% of bosses think their employees are satisfied. Only 50% of employees agreed, while the other 50% reported dissatisfaction with their jobs.

Commitment
32% vs 12%

32% of employees are actively seeking to leave their job, while only 12% are deeply committed to staying. However, 31% of bosses think their employees are deeply committed to staying; 13% think their employees are actively seeking to leave.

Active Employee Job Searching
41% vs 42%

41% of employees say that it is very likely that they will actually search for a new job within the next 3 months. Employers hold opposite opinions – 42% think that it is very unlikely that their employees will search for different jobs in the near future.

Desired Benefits
35% vs 5%

35% of employees want the ability to work from home, but only 5% of employers allow it.

45% of employees want professional development opportunities. Among employers, professional development was not even mentioned or thought of as a benefit.

Q. What strategies could be implemented to bridge these communication gaps? Explain.

Job Satisfaction

7. Cultural Discussion Questions

Read the passage and talk about the questions in as much detail as possible.

Incentives

In order to improve employee morale, many companies introduce incentives to increase the productivity of their workers. Some of these companies give opportunities for their employees to build rapport with one another outside of the office through team building activities and meals. Others provide perks, like company stock shares, free meals, and complementary services that employees and their families can enjoy. Still, others appeal to their employees' competitive natures by offering incentives to their top performers.

1. What does your company do to raise morale?
2. In your opinion, which is the best strategy to improve the performance and morale of workers?

Reading Employees' Minds

Studies have shown that happy and engaged member of an organization tend to be more successful and innovative in the workplace, A **TIME magazine** survey discovered that **less than half** of American workers are satisfied with their jobs and that focusing on employee satisfaction may lead to greater productivity and profitability. According to a study of US employees, **job security** is the most important aspect of employee happiness.

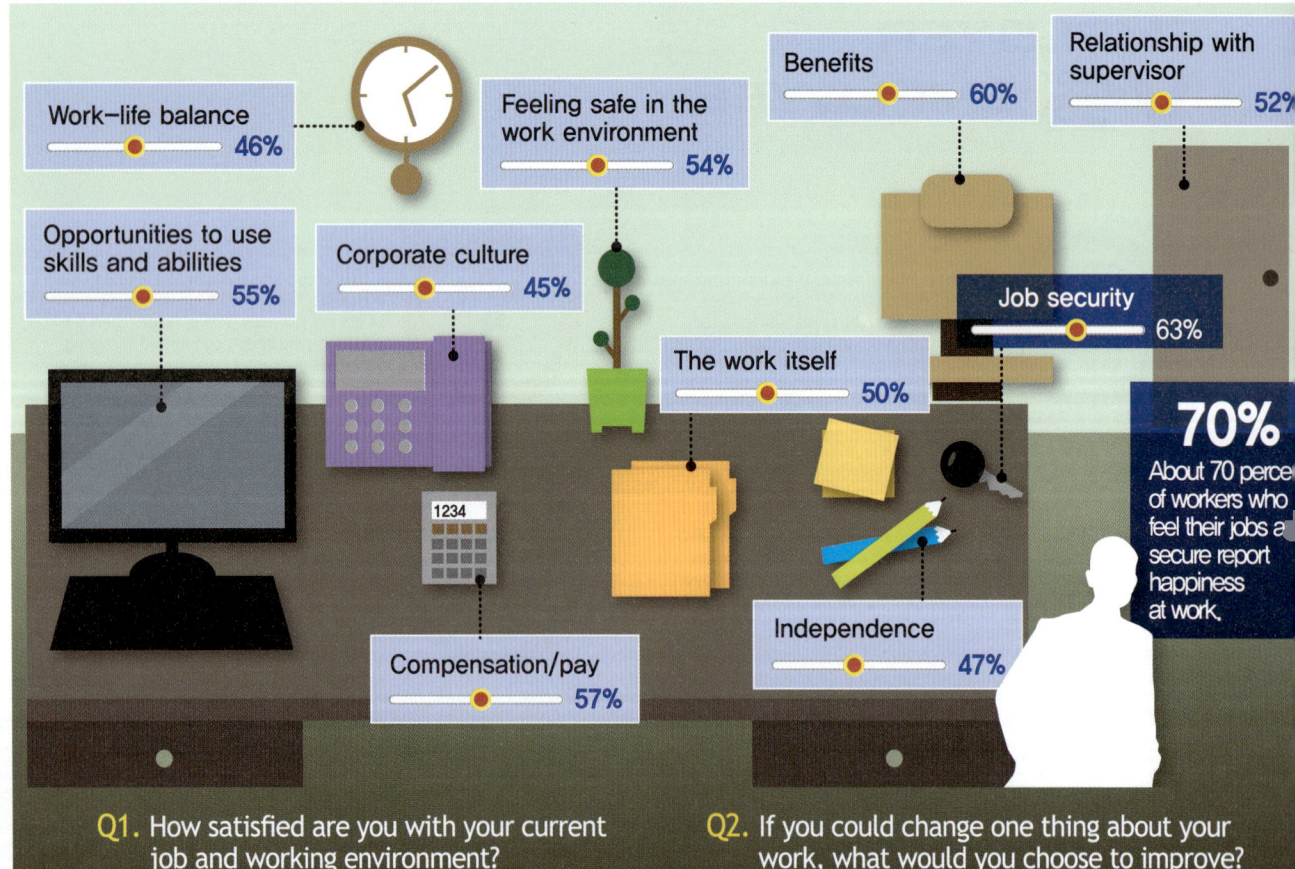

- Work–life balance 46%
- Opportunities to use skills and abilities 55%
- Feeling safe in the work environment 54%
- Corporate culture 45%
- Benefits 60%
- Relationship with supervisor 52%
- Job security 63%
- The work itself 50%
- Compensation/pay 57%
- Independence 47%

70% About 70 percent of workers who feel their jobs are secure report happiness at work.

Q1. How satisfied are you with your current job and working environment?

Q2. If you could change one thing about your work, what would you choose to improve?

Lesson 11 / Job Satisfaction   75

8. If You Ask Me

Read the discussion topic and select the statement that you believe in the most. Then role-play the scenario.

Lifetime Employment

Historically, the first job you got was the start of a lifelong career. Even after the Industrial Revolution, the trend still continued as people moved into cities to take advantage of increased employment opportunities. Until relatively recently, it was common for people to spend their entire lives employed by the same company. In recent years, however, permanent employment for life has become harder for companies to promise. With a shortage of available jobs in specific fields, more and more people nowadays find that they might have to change careers multiple times during their lifetimes. Because of this, many fear that their dream of retirement will not be possible because the perks of working full-time at a single employer for life have disappeared.

Topic Question
Should permanent lifetime employment be guaranteed to new hires?

Supportive Opinion VS **Non-Supportive Opinion**

Role-play

Act out the role-play using the slang and idioms and useful expressions.

Situation
You are visiting a therapist to talk about your stressful workplace. Lately, you feel that you can't escape the pressure even when you punch out. Most of the stress is due to your boss. He never takes responsibility for his actions, constantly leaves the office for personal reasons, makes lazy mistakes that he expects others to catch, and always expects the team to pick up the slack. In addition, he is horrible at prioritizing tasks, so he often has to stay late. This is a problem for you because nobody is allowed to leave the office until he does. Tell the therapist about your problem and ask for his or her advice.

Role A
- Tell the therapist about your work life.
- Explain how the situation makes you feel.

Role B
- Sympathize that the situation is unfair.
- Encourage your patient to search for another job with better conditions.

Wrapping Up!
Tell four things that you learned from this lesson and review.

1.
2.
3.
4.

12 I'd Like to Report a Break-in

Learning Objective

Upon completion of this lesson, you will be able to **discuss home invasions and how to prevent them.**

Expression Check

- ✓ I think someone has just broken into my house.
- ✓ They made off with everything.
- ✓ The police have been dispatched to your location.

1. Warm Up Activity

Talk about the questions.

1. Is there much crime in your neighborhood?
2. Have you or someone you know ever been a victim of a break-in?
3. Do you think theft is ever justified, for example, if someone steals food because they are starving?

2. Useful Phrases

Match the phrases (a-d) to the phrases (1-4) to form a complete sentence. The useful phrases are italicized.

A. They *made off with*

B. *How on earth* did they break in?

C. Everything is gone.

D. If the *security system is triggered,*

1. They completely *cleaned us out.*
2. *everything but the kitchen sink.*
3. a security team is *automatically dispatched.*
4. I thought I *armed the alarm.*

3. Slang & Idioms

Check out the slang and idioms and try to make your own sentences.

A caught red-handed : found in the act of doing something wrong	*Officers arrived and caught him red-handed with the stolen goods.*
B on the run : trying to avoid being captured	*The escaped convicts are currently still on the run from the law.*
C clean out : steal or take everything from (someone or something)	*The thieves cleaned out all the valuables from the store.*
D break in : force entry into a building or home	*We believe that the thief broke in shortly after midnight.*

4. Key Conversation

Read through the dialogue and practice with a partner.

Did You Hear That?

Brenda (whispering) Jerry! Jerry, wake up! I think I heard someone in the house!

Jerry Huh? What's the problem? Why aren't you asleep?

Brenda Shh! I think an intruder has broken into the house. Do something!

Jerry What do you want me to do? Give me your phone. I'll call 911, and the police will be here soon.

Brenda Shh, listen! Did you hear that? Go look and see!

Jerry The worst thing to do is to surprise a burglar. The police will be here soon. Let them do their job. Hopefully, they'll catch the burglar red-handed.

Brenda What if they clean us out?

Jerry Don't worry; we're insured. Listen! Sirens... it's the police! Have you ever seen anyone being caught red-handed? Well, now's the time.

Brenda I think we'd better just stay out of the way. Whoever they are, they're probably already on the run. Besides, what if they're armed?

Jerry Hey, you have no faith in our police force! Besides, you were just telling me to go and take a look! C'mon! Let's go and watch!

Questions

1. In your opinion, were Brenda and Jerry scared during the break-in?
2. Do you think Jerry should have gone to check on the noises before calling 911?

I'd Like to Report a Break-in

How to Protect Children from Predators

Always
- Keep children with you at all times.
- Accompany and supervise children in public facilities.
- Have a plan in case you become separated, including a pre-designated spot to meet.
- Teach children to look for people who can help.
- Remind children to remain in the area where they become separated.
- Turn shopping trips into opportunities to practice safe shopping skills.

Never
- Dress children in clothing that displays their first or last names.
- Leave children in toy stores or public facilities expecting supervision from store personnel.
- Go shopping or attend a public event with a child if you feel you are going to be distracted.
- Allow younger children to shop on their own to purchase surprise gifts for friends or family.
- Drop off older children at a mall or public place without agreeing on a clear plan for picking them up.

Q1. What safe habits do you teach your child?
Q2. Why do you think they are important?

5. Situational Collocations

Complete the sentences using the collocations from the word box.

Word Box
- discourage intruders
- stash a spare key
- face resistance
- counter any threat
- triggered an alarm
- the most opportune time
- forced his way into
- breaking and entering

1. Burglars tend to choose times when they are less likely to _____.
2. I always _____ under a rock by the door.
3. It seems like they were waiting for _____ to break in.
4. They'll be looking to _____ they might face.
5. Leave a light on to _____ when you know you will be away for a while.
6. The broken window _____ and the police were notified.
7. The thief _____ the empty home.
8. He was arrested last night for _____.

6. What Would You Do?

Read the situation and explain what you would do in that situation.

A Homecoming Surprise

You arrive home after a weekend seminar, and you are very tired. All you can think of is a hot cup of tea and your nice, comfortable bed. You open your front door, turn on the light, and see that your apartment has been trashed and everything has been taken, but the kitchen sink. You call the police, who examine everything. A few days later, you get a call from the police, who tell you they have caught the burglar red-handed trying to pawn your watch. When you arrive at the police station to press charges, you discover that the burglar is your building superintendent.

Q1. Would you press charges? Why or why not?

Q2. If you could confront him, what would you say to your building superintendent?

Q3. Would you tell the rest of the tenants in your building? Why or why not?

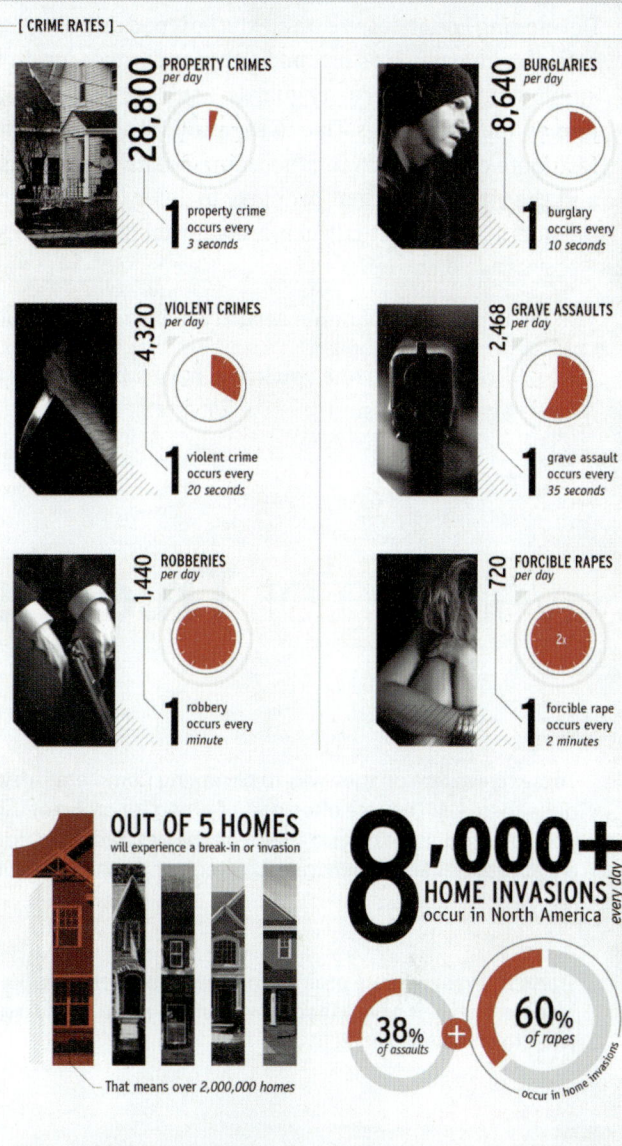

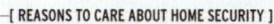

Q1 Have you ever experienced a home invasion?

Q2 What are some things that you can do to protect your home and property from robbers?

I'd Like to Report a Break-in

7. Cultural Discussion Questions

Read the passage and talk about the questions in as much detail as possible.

Beware of the Snake

Developing countries are often stereotyped as being dangerous. This view often stems from the higher rate of crimes, such as pickpocketing and break-ins. In these countries, wealthy inhabitants often employ individual security guards, use a security service, or install alarm systems to protect their homes and belongings. Due to the prohibitive cost of these security measures, a large number of less fortunate citizens turn to other more creative solutions, like keeping animals such as dogs, geese, and even snakes on their property to deter would-be thieves. These animals are able to frighten off intruders and are actually a more affordable and safer solution than keeping weapons like firearms.

1. What kinds of home security measures are most popular in your country?
2. Do you or anyone you know have a pet in your home or on your property to provide security against intrusion?

Evolution of Thieves

Targeted Thieves

These thieves are on their way to becoming Complete Thieves but they are NOT quite there yet. They are often part of a "ring," or group of thieves, where they are able to get information and advice on the best tactics to rip off their victims. They are able to quickly identify valuable items and can find security systems.

Prowler Thieves

These thieves are more professional than Smasher or Opportunity Thieves. They will have a more developed plan on what to grab and what to do with stolen items.

Smasher Thieves

These thieves burglarize because they need money. Usually, they are on drugs, or they are very poor.

Opportunity Thieves

These thieves do not have a plan. If they see doors unlocked and see stranded bags lying around, they will pick them up, invade your house, and steal your things.

Born to Steal

Complete Thieves

These thieves are experts in their field. They know practically everything about the value of specific items and security locks. Many manage their own rings of associates and they are able to navigate the system with ease.

Q. Which kinds of thieves are most common in your country? Explain.

8. If You Ask Me

Read the discussion topic and select the statement that you believe in the most. Then role-play the scenario.

An Eye for an Eye

Each country has its own unique legal system in which legislators define crimes and set fitting punishments. What is illegal in one country may be perfectly acceptable in another, and punishments for identical crimes can vary from a simple fine to the death penalty. In some countries, capital punishment has been outlawed while in others, criminals can be executed for seemingly minor crimes. Furthermore, some countries, like the US, allow each state or province to set its own standard regarding crime and punishment.

Topic Question

Do you think all countries should have the same standard punishments for specific crimes?

Supportive Opinion VS **Non-Supportive Opinion**

Role-play

Act out the role-play using the slang and idioms and useful expressions.

Situation

You are currently visiting your sibling who lives in a brand new, state-of-the-art apartment building. The property boasts tight security with alarm systems in every unit and an around-the-clock security guard on call. One afternoon, you are taking a nap alone in the apartment when you are woken up by a strange noise coming from another room. You are convinced that there is an intruder in the apartment. Call your brother or sister to ask what to do.

Role A
- Explain the situation to your sibling.
- Ask what you need to do to activate the alarm.

Role B
- Assure your sibling it is probably nothing.
- Tell him or her to lock the bedroom door and push the panic button to call security.

Wrapping Up!
Tell four things that you learned from this lesson and review.

1.
2.
3.
4.

New Get Up To Speed+ Book 8
SLANG & IDIOM GLOSSARY

Lesson 1

on cloud nine	extremely happy, joyful
over the moon	experiencing happiness beyond your imagination
Pinch me.	when something is so good that you must be dreaming
tickled pink	extremely happy or amused

Lesson 2

near-death experience	an experience described by some people who have been close to death
not a chance	not possible
one in a million	a chance that is extremely unlikely
work miracles	achieve extraordinary results, especially in trying to improve a situation

Lesson 3

15 minutes of fame	a short lived media publicity or celebrity
having a field day	busy doing something that they enjoy
rumor mill	the process by which rumors and gossip start and spread
star-studded	including many famous people

Lesson 4

be laid off	losing one's job because a company lacks work or funds to pay your salary
down in the dumps	in a gloomy or depressed mood
temporary setback	a defeat or reverse of progress
Things are falling into place.	used when things are happening in a satisfactory way, without problems

Lesson 5

at one's wits' end	at the limits of one's emotional or mental limitations
between a rock and a hard place	in a situation where one is faced with two equally difficult alternatives
let off steam	get rid of pent-up energy or strong emotion
stressed out	tired and irritable because of too much work or pressure

Lesson 6

global village	a concept considering the world to be a single community linked by telecommunications
glocal	something that is both global and local
become a worldwide phenomenon	to spread quickly globally
butterfly effect	the idea that a very small action can cause a chain of events that has large implications

Lesson 7

politically correct	extremely careful not to offend or upset any group of people in society who have a disadvantage
racial slur	a negative term used to refer to a particular race of people
stick out like a sore thumb	be obviously different from the surrounding people or things
the wrong side of the tracks	a part of a town that is considered poor and dangerous

Lesson 8

apple-polish	someone who utilizes gifts and flattery as a means of gaining favor
backhanded compliments	a remark which seems to be a compliment but could also be understood as an insult
butter someone up	praise or flatter someone in order to make him or her more receptive or willing
fish for a compliment	try to make someone say something nice about you, usually by first criticizing yourself

Lesson 9

battle of wills	a confilct, argument or struggle where both sides are determined to win at all costs
let sleeping dogs lie	avoid interfering in a situation that is currently causing no problems
pushover	a person who is easy to overcome or influence
take the bull by the horns	deal directly and decisively with a difficult, dangerous, or unpleasant situation

Lesson 10

cross that bridge when I come to it	deal with a problem when and if it arises
government issued ID	any official document which may be used to prove a person's identity
Green Card	an ID card carried by a permanent resident of the US
rocky road	have difficulties or problems to deal with

Lesson 11

perks	money, goods, or other benefits an employee receives
pick up the slack	do the work that someone else has stopped doing but still needs to be done
punch in / out	record the time of one's arrival or departure at work
slave driver	a person who works others very hard

Lesson 12

break in	force entry into a building or home
caught red-handed	found in the act of doing something wrong
clean out	steal or take everything from (someone or something)
on the run	trying to avoid being captured

New Get Up To Speed+ Book 8
ANSWER KEY

Lesson 1

Useful Phrases

a   3
b   1
c   4
d   2

Situational Collocations

1   financially free
2   just what I needed
3   significant breakthrough
4   purely by chance
5   good fortune
6   unexpected windfall
7   happy dance
8   extremely lucky

Lesson 2

Useful Phrases

a   4
b   2
c   3
d   1

Situational Collocations

1   unlikely chain of events
2   implausible story
3   statistically improbable
4   unthinkable coincidence
5   beyond reason
6   no small feat
7   bewildering explanation
8   mind-blowing ending

Lesson 3

Useful Phrases

a   3
b   1
c   2
d   4

Situational Collocations

1   story going around
2   Keep this to yourself
3   vicious rumor
4   unfounded suspicion
5   unsubstantiated allegations
6   Rumor has it
7   acting scandalously
8   malicious gossip

Lesson 4

Useful Phrases

a   2
b   4
c   3
d   1

Situational Collocations

1   fall into depression
2   put on a brave face
3   bury your feelings
4   coping strategy
5   process this information
6   grieve the loss
7   a range of emotions
8   gave me insight

Lesson 5

Useful Phrases

a   4
b   1 or 3
c   1 or 3
d   2

Situational Collocations

1. make time for
2. pare down
3. enough hours in the day
4. relinquishing control
5. undue stress
6. common theme
7. identify the source
8. debilitating anxiety

Lesson 6

Useful Phrases

a 2
b 4
c 1
d 3

Situational Collocations

1. unprecedented feat
2. much-needed support
3. what is at stake
4. competitive pressure
5. allocation of resources
6. impose our standards
7. vital benefits
8. Emerging market economies

Lesson 7

Useful Phrases

a 2
b 4
c 1
d 3

Situational Collocations

1. Reverse discrimination
2. public sentiment
3. belittling remarks
4. misogynist attitude
5. hit a nerve
6. narrow-minded view
7. raise awareness
8. clear bias

Lesson 8

Useful Phrases

a 3
b 1
c 4
d 2

Situational Collocations

1. an obvious suck-up
2. thinly veiled criticism
3. sincere admiration
4. hidden agenda
5. rubs me the wrong way
6. a genuine compliment
7. from the heart
8. lavish him with compliments

Lesson 9

Useful Phrases

a 2
b 4
c 1
d 3

Situational Collocations

1. stubborn pride
2. awkward silence
3. a low blow
4. a shouting match
5. butting heads
6. make a case for

New Get Up To Speed+ Book 8
ANSWER KEY

7 disrespectful attitude
8 seething with rage

Lesson 10

Useful Phrases

a 4
b 2
c 1
d 3

Situational Collocations

1 keep track of
2 left it behind
3 claim lost articles
4 mild annoyance
5 report my loss
6 careless mistake
7 seemed out of it
8 lose sight of

Lesson 11

Useful Phrases

a 2
b 4
c 1
d 3

Situational Collocations

1 gives a voice to
2 toxic work environment
3 create synergy
4 drives bottom-line results
5 a clear path for
6 collective bargaining power
7 innate strengths
8 impact focus

Lesson 12

Useful Phrases

a 2
b 4
c 1
d 3

Situational Collocations

1 face resistance
2 stash a spare key
3 the most opportune time
4 counter any threat
5 discourage intruders
6 triggered an alarm
7 forced his way into
8 breaking and entering